Nature-Inspired Optimization Algorithms with Java

A Look at Optimization Techniques

Shashank Jain

Apress®

Nature-Inspired Optimization Algorithms with Java: A Look at Optimization Techniques

Shashank Jain
Bangalore, India

ISBN-13 (pbk): 978-1-4842-7400-2   ISBN-13 (electronic): 978-1-4842-7401-9
https://doi.org/10.1007/978-1-4842-7401-9

Managing Director, Apress Media LLC: Welmoed Spahr
Acquisitions Editor: Celestin Suresh John
Development Editor: James Markham
Coordinating Editor: Shrikant Vishwakarma

Cover designed by eStudioCalamar

Cover image designed by Pexels

Distributed to the book trade worldwide by Springer Science+Business Media LLC, 1 New York Plaza, Suite 4600, New York, NY 10004. Phone 1-800-SPRINGER, fax (201) 348-4505, e-mail orders-ny@springer-sbm.com, or visit www.springeronline.com. Apress Media, LLC is a California LLC and the sole member (owner) is Springer Science + Business Media Finance Inc (SSBM Finance Inc). SSBM Finance Inc is a **Delaware** corporation.

For information on translations, please e-mail booktranslations@springernature.com; for reprint, paperback, or audio rights, please e-mail bookpermissions@springernature.com.

Apress titles may be purchased in bulk for academic, corporate, or promotional use. eBook versions and licenses are also available for most titles. For more information, reference our Print and eBook Bulk Sales web page at http://www.apress.com/bulk-sales.

Any source code or other supplementary material referenced by the author in this book is available to readers on GitHub via the book's product page, located at www.apress.com/978-1-4842-7400-2. For more detailed information, please visit http://www.apress.com/source-code.

Printed on acid-free paper

This small book is dedicated to my parents, my wife Manisha, and my daughter Isha. Without the support of each one of them, I would not have been able to write this book.

Table of Contents

About the Author

Shashank Jain has worked in the IT industry for 20 years, mainly in cloud computing and distributed systems. He has a keen interest in virtualization techniques, security, and complex systems.

Shashank has several software patents in cloud computing, IoT, and machine learning. He has been a speaker at many cloud conferences. In addition, he holds Sun, Microsoft, and Linux kernel certifications. He is also the author of the book *Linux Containers and Virtualization* (Apress, 2020).

About the Technical Reviewer

Prudhvi Potuganti is a data scientist and educator with more than six years of experience in forecasting, optimization, machine learning, natural language processing in web, marketing, e-commerce domains, and electrical utilities. He has extensive experience building algorithms from scratch to suit client requirements and has published his work in reputed journals and conferences with over 60 citations to date.

Prudhvi works at supervisedlearning.com, creating industry-relevant AI, data science, ML, NLP, and optimization courses. He has mentored over 1000 students in the data science domain. He graduated from NIT Warangal with a gold medal for Excellence in Research.

Prudhvi believes in the power of data-based decision-making, data-driven business. With a mission to make positivity viral, his team built an AI engine to predict heart-warming and inspiring stories @ The Positive India.

Introduction

The great scientist and science communicator Carl Sagan said, "I don't want to believe. I want to know." Taking these words as inspiration, this book sets out to explore the wonderful world of nature-inspired metaheuristic algorithms. The book covers the basics of nature-inspired algorithms, including whale optimization, gray wolf optimization, bat optimization, cuckoo search, and particle swarm optimization. The book explains each algorithm with pseudocode and uses Java code examples to explore these algorithms.

CHAPTER 1

Introduction to Optimization: Problems and Techniques

> *True optimization is the revolutionary contribution of modern research to the decision process.*
>
> —George Dantzig, American scientist

This chapter introduces the optimization techniques, focusing on those that are metaheuristic/nature-inspired. You learn how to benchmark these techniques and the types of benchmark functions that are available.

Optimization at a Glance

Every day in business, government, and our personal lives, we decide how to best use available resources, including time and money. It can be difficult to decide which items to buy or which routes to take to work.

© Shashank Jain 2022
S. Jain, *Nature-Inspired Optimization Algorithms with Java*,
https://doi.org/10.1007/978-1-4842-7401-9_1

For organizations dealing with supply chains, this challenge is worse. For example, they must address how to load packages on a fleet of trucks, which routes drivers should take to make deliveries in the least amount time, or how to assign crews and aircraft to airline flights as they move across the country throughout the day.

Decisions on allocating limited resources to different uses when there are many options and interrelationships are prime candidates for optimization. In optimization, you need to quantitatively define a model that specifies all the ways, times, or places your resources may be allocated and all the significant constraints on resources and uses that must be met. Then determine the solution that meets the best allocation of resources.

In general, optimization problems are based on three basic tenets.

- Decision variables

- The objective function

- Constraints

Quantified decision variables are the number of resources allocated to each use; for example, the number of employees working each shift or the number of packages loaded onto each truck. To determine what best means, you must define a quantity called the *objective* that can calculate the value of the decision variables—such as minimizing costs, maximizing profits, or minimizing production time.

Since any resource is subject to some limitations, to complete the model, you must define each constraint or limit the ways resources may be allocated that reflect real-world situations. Usually, these are simple constraint limits calculated from the decision variables, such as "a maximum of 150 hours to complete the tasks."

For example, a shopkeeper wants to keep items that maximize profit or to lower inventory costs. In this case, the decision variables are the items to keep. A constraint might be the amount of capital. Profit is the objective function.

Another example is a stock investment portfolio. The objective function is to maximize wealth. The decision variables are the individual stocks. A constraint is the amount of money the investor has.

An optimization problem can be solved in two main ways: *exact methods* and *heuristic methods*.

The beauty of exact optimization methods comes from a guaranteed identification of the best solution (technically, an optimal solution). But depending on the problem sets, the optimal solution could be costly, time-consuming, or impractical. If the decision variable space is too big, exact method optimization may be intractable.

In such cases, it's better to use heuristic methods, which usually provide good, quick solutions. Heuristics are often the key to solving the most difficult business problems in constrained timeframes.

You now see the kinds of optimization problems we face in our daily lives and work.

Optimization Problems

Optimization problems can be broadly classified into five types. If a problem is linear, the constraints and objective function can only be linear. In *nonlinear* problems, the constraints and objective functions can either be linear or nonlinear. When the decision variables are not mentioned, they are assumed to be *continuous*. In *integer programming*, the decision variables are discrete. In *mixed-integer programming,* the decision variables can be continuous and discrete. These optimization problems are further described in Table 1-1.

Table 1-1. *Problems Associated with Optimization*

Type	Decision Variable		Constraints		Objective Function	
	Continuous	**Discrete**	**Linear**	**Nonlinear**	**Linear**	**Nonlinear**
Linear Programming	Yes	No	Yes	No	Yes	No
Nonlinear Programming	Yes	No	Yes	Yes	Yes	Yes
Integer Linear Programming	No	Yes	Yes	No	Yes	No
Mixed-Integer Linear Programming	Yes	Yes	Yes	No	Yes	No
Mixed-Integer Nonlinear Programming	Yes	Yes	Yes	Yes	Yes	Yes

Optimization Techniques

There are three types of optimization techniques to solve optimization problems.

- **Mathematical techniques** are based on the problem's geometrical properties.

  Examples include the simplex algorithm for integer programming, where constraints and objective function are linear; the branch-and-bound method for mixed-integer linear programming; and the steepest descent method and Newton's method for nonlinear programming.

- **Metaheuristic techniques** are based on approximate solutions and are mostly inspired by natural processes.

  Examples of metaheuristic techniques include particle swarm optimization, gray wolf optimization, and ant colony optimization.

  The beauty of a metaheuristic technique is that it doesn't depend on the structure of the problem. The way to solve a linear programming problem is the same as solving a nonlinear programming problem. For this reason, these techniques are also known as *black-box optimization techniques.*

- Other techniques include the Fibonacci method and the golden-section method.

This book focuses on metaheuristic techniques. The exploration of the other techniques is left to you, the reader.

> *Optimization hinders evolution. Everything should be built top-down, except the first time. Simplicity does not precede complexity but follows it.*

> — Alan Perlis

Metaheuristic Techniques for Optimization

Metaheuristic techniques are inspired by nature and natural processes. Most techniques are based on principles of self-organization and emergence.

Nature is full of examples of emergence. The two great laws of physics—thermodynamics and general relativity—are examples of emergent behavior. Take temperature as an example. It's the result of many molecules interacting vigorously with each other. General relativity states that space-time is a curve. Gravity is a result of a curve in space and time. What causes it? Scientists grapple with defining a quantum view of gravity.

But what is emergence? Let's explore.

Two scientific models define all the things, behaviors, and processes around us. These processes range from plants to animals to humans in a social network.

Reductionism and Emergence

Let's look at a simple phenomenon—water. The hierarchy is made of molecules, atoms, electrons, protons, and neutrons and quarks at the quantum level. There are two different scales for viewing a thing. In physics, this is called renormalization. Since the number of molecules in an object is too high to count and each molecule has a high degree of freedom, it is difficult to tell the whole from the part.

Let's look at the properties of an object at two scales.

- **Microscopic** describes the properties of individual particles, such as mass, velocity, and position.

- **Macroscopic** describes properties like pressure and temperature.

The "whole from the part" means that we look at each molecule in a subpart and then compute the behavior/property of the complete system. This is a reductionist approach: break up the system into its lowest level and start from there.

John Wheeler, an influential Princeton University physicist whose work touched on topics from nuclear physics to black holes, expressed an interesting alternative: "Every law of physics pushed to the extreme will be found to be statistical and approximate, not mathematically perfect and precise." This means that aggregation is done at every level or scale. This is also known as *renormalization*. This mathematical formalism systematically goes from the small to the large. The essential step is to take averages. The emergent model doesn't go into microscopic details but describes the collective behavior that emerges. A classic example is human intelligence based on the interaction of neurons. An individual neuron is very simple (it either fires or doesn't fire).

The interaction between multiple neurons gives rise to intelligence and perception, or you can say that intelligence emerges. Nature has tons of examples of emergence—ant colonies, bird swarms, honey bees. A single ant, for example, has very limited capabilities, but when in a group, a collective behavior emerges, which helps ants in tasks like foraging.

Ants are relatively simple components in the complex system of the ant colony. Or, more specifically, each ant component's behavior is relatively simple compared to what the overall system is doing. An ant colony can engage in complex behaviors like building nests, foraging for food, raising aphid "livestock," waging war with other colonies, and burying their dead. In contrast, no one single has the impulse or knowledge to undertake such collective tasks independently. Collective behaviors that arise unexpectedly are called *emergent* behaviors.

The individual elements follow some well-defined rules of interaction, and complex behavior emerges. The Internet and social networks are examples of emergent systems. Computer science studies that try to model the human brain via neural networks or nature-inspired algorithms are all cases of emergence in computer science.

Self-Organization

Self-organization is a principle of complex adaptive systems that explain collective behavior. Think of them as emergent systems with a feedback loop that constantly allows the adjustments at the micro level. The parts of a system organize themselves according to the information perceived from the environment and the simple principles they obey together. When the principles are functional and unambiguous to everyone, the system self-organizes. The team becomes more than the sum of its parts and has *emergent* properties that the individuals do not have.

> *According to the systems view, the essential properties of an organism or living system are properties of the whole, which none of the parts have. They arise from the interactions and relationships among the parts. These properties are destroyed when the system is dissected, either physically or theoretically, into isolated elements. Although we can discern individual parts in any system, these parts are not isolated, and the nature of the whole is always different from the mere sum of its parts.*
>
> —Fritjof Capra, *The Web of Life*

Metaheuristic techniques are the techniques that, instead of depending on the shape of a problem (like a mathematical property), treat optimization more like a black box. Applying this technique leads to finding an approximate solution in a large search space where normal techniques easily become compute-intensive and even intractable.

Exploration vs. Exploitation

In upcoming chapters, you encounter exploration and exploitation and look at how nature uses these mechanisms to arrive at an optimal solution.

Exploration means exploring new solutions. For example, in day-to-day life, we generally try to learn new things. We keep exploring the world to find new solutions to our problems or increase our knowledge. Animals similarly explore new solutions to accomplish certain tasks.

On the other hand, *exploitation* means using an existing solution or something in the near vicinity. It optimizes known solutions and knowledge.

There is always a trade-off between exploration and exploitation in which a mix of both strategies is needed to arrive at a good solution. Exploration and exploitation are best understood under the umbrella of multiarmed bandit problems (see `https://en.wikipedia.org/wiki/Multi-armed_bandit`).

Workflow for Metaheuristic Techniques

The following terms are all part of the metaheuristic technique workflow, so it's important to put them in context before reviewing the process.

- A **solution** represents the dimensions or features of an individual.

- A **population** is a collection of individual solutions.

- **Parameters** can be adjusted/fine-tuned for specific algorithms.

- The **fitness** function is the objective function that needs to be optimized.

- **Iterations/generations** are the number of iterations to arrive at an optimal or best solution.

The following describes the workflow process.

1. Define parameters of the problem, such as population size and the number of iterations.

2. Generate a population of random solutions.

3. Iterate.

4. Select some solutions from the population.

5. Vary the solutions a bit.

6. Check the fitness of the solutions obtained in step 5.

7. Apply a survivor function to take the best solutions.

8. Go to step 3. (Keep doing this until you reach the maximum number of iterations).

Benchmark Functions for Metaheuristic Techniques

Benchmark functions test the performance of metaheuristic algorithms. Algorithms that perform well in benchmark functions tend to perform well in real-world problems. There are plenty of benchmark functions. Table 1-2 lists a few of them. Some of them are used in the algorithms discussed in the coming chapters.

Table 1-2. *Benchmark Functions*

Name	Plot	Formula
Rastrigin function		$f(\mathbf{x}) = An + \sum_{i=1}^{n} \left[x_i^2 - A \cos(2\pi x_i) \right]$ where: $A = 10$
Ackley function		$f(x, y) = -20 \exp\left[-0.2\sqrt{0.5\left(x^2 + y^2\right)} \right]$ $- \exp[0.5\left(\cos 2\pi x + \cos 2\pi y\right)] + e + 20$
Sphere Function		$f(x) = \sum_{i=1}^{n} x_i^2$
Booth Function		$f(x, y) = \left(x + 2y - 7\right)^2 + \left(2x + y - 5\right)^2$
Levi Function N.13		$f(x, y) = \sin^2 3\pi x + \left(x - 1\right)^2 \left(1 + \sin^2 3\pi y\right)$ $+ \left(y - 1\right)^2 \left(1 + \sin^2 2\pi y\right)$

Summary

This chapter discussed optimization and various techniques involved in solving optimization problems. It introduced the metaheuristic way of solving optimization problems and described some benchmark functions that metaheuristic algorithms are evaluated against.

CHAPTER 2

Mammals: Whale, Gray Wolf, and Bat Optimization

This chapter introduces you to the world of optimization problem-solving by looking at whales, gray wolves, and bats. You learn how these mammals have developed specific techniques for attacking certain problems they need to solve for survival. These problems include foraging for food or hunting.

History: Whales

The whales do not sing because they have an answer. They sing because they have a song.

—Gregory Colbert, Canadian filmmaker

Whales are the biggest mammals in the world. They can grow up to 30 meters in length and weigh up to 180 tons. There are many different species of whales, including killer, minke, sei, humpback, right, finback, and blue.

© Shashank Jain 2022
S. Jain, *Nature-Inspired Optimization Algorithms with Java*,
https://doi.org/10.1007/978-1-4842-7401-9_2

Whales are predatory mammals with high intelligence and a high emotional quotient.

According to research, whales have cells in certain areas of their brains that are similar to those of humans. These *spindle cells* are responsible for the power of judgment, emotions, and social behaviors. A whale has almost twice the number of these cells as an adult human, which is one of the main reasons for their intelligence. It has been proven that whales can think, learn, judge, communicate, and become as emotional as humans can, although with a much lower level of intelligence. Whales are also social. Some of their species (killer whales, for instance) can live in a family for their entire lives.

This chapter focuses on humpback whales (*Megaptera novaeangliae*), one of the biggest baleen whales.

The most interesting thing about humpback whales is their special hunting method. This foraging behavior is called the *bubble-net feeding method*. Humpback whales prefer to hunt schools of krill or small fishes close to the surface. It has been observed that this foraging is done by creating distinctive bubbles along a circle or a 9-shaped path. Before 2011, this behavior had only been observed from the surface. However, Goldbogen et al. [4] investigated this behavior using tag sensors. They captured 300 tag-derived bubble-net feeding events of nine individual humpback whales. They found two maneuvers associated with bubbles and named them *upward spirals* and *double loops*. In an upward-spiral maneuver, humpback whales dive down about 12 meters, create a spiral-shaped bubble around the prey, and then swim up toward the surface. The double-loop maneuver includes three different stages: coral loop, lobtail, and capture loop.

It is worth mentioning that bubble-net feeding is a unique behavior that can only be observed in humpback whales. A mathematical model for the spiral bubble-net feeding maneuver is used to perform optimization.

Bubble-net feeding is when whales deliberately blow bubbles from their noses to encircle their food (krill and fish) like a net to concentrate their prey into a tight ball. Then, the whale or group of whales swim together from beneath this ball, rise toward the surface, open their mouths, and gulp up their prey.

The whale optimization algorithm (WOA) is a recently developed swarm-based metaheuristic algorithm based on the bubble-net hunting maneuver technique for solving complex optimization problems. It has been a widely accepted swarm intelligence technique in various engineering fields due to its simple structure, less required operator, fast convergence speed, and better balancing capability between exploration and exploitation phases. Owing to its optimal performance and efficiency, the algorithm's applications are extensively used in multidisciplinary fields.

Whale optimization is based on two strategies.

- Exploration (encircling)

- Exploitation (attack using bubble-net methods)

Encircling Prey

Let's discuss some of the characteristics that whales display when encircling the prey.

- Humpback whales know the location of prey and encircle them.

- They consider the current best-candidate solution as the best-obtained and near-optimal solution.

- After assigning the best-candidate solution, the other
  agents update their positions toward the best search
  agent, as shown in Equation 2-1.

$$D = |C \cdot X^*(t) - X(t)|$$

$$X(t+1) = X^*(t) - A \cdot D$$

Equation 2-1. *Position updating for whales*

In Equation 2-1, t is the current iteration, A and C are coefficient vectors, X^* is the position vector of the best solution, X indicates the position vector of a solution, and $||$ is the absolute value.

The A and C vectors are calculated as shown in Equation 2-2.

$$A = 2a \cdot r \cdot a$$

$$C = 2 \cdot r$$

Equation 2-2. *Calculating the coefficient vectors*

The components of a linearly decrease from 2 to 0 throughout iterations, and r is a random vector in $[0; 1]$.

Exploitation Phase: Bubble-Net Attacking Method

Humpback whales attack their prey using the bubble-net mechanism. This mechanism is mathematically formulated by shrinking the encircling mechanism.

In this mechanism, A is a random value in the interval $[-a, a]$. The value of a decreases from 2 to 0 throughout the iterations. Then, the position of the whale is updated in a spiral fashion. This is based on the distance between the whale's location and the prey's location and is calculated based on two equal probability equations (see Equations 2-3 and 2-4).

$$X(t+1) = X_{rand}\ (t) - A \bullet D\ (p<0.5)$$
$$X(t+1) = D' \bullet e^{bl} \bullet \cos(27d) + X^*(t)\ (p>0.5)$$

Equation 2-3. *Bubble-net mechanism*

D' is the distance between the prey and the whale.

$$D' = |\,X^*(t) = X(t)\,|$$

Equation 2-4. *Distance update between prey and whale*

Whale Flowchart

Figure 2-1 depicts the flow of the whale optimization algorithm. It starts by initializing parameters such as population size and the number of iterations. It initializes the population itself, and then during each iteration, it updates the position of each of the agents (member of population) and calculates the fitness of each agent. After the last iteration, the agent that best fits is considered the best solution.

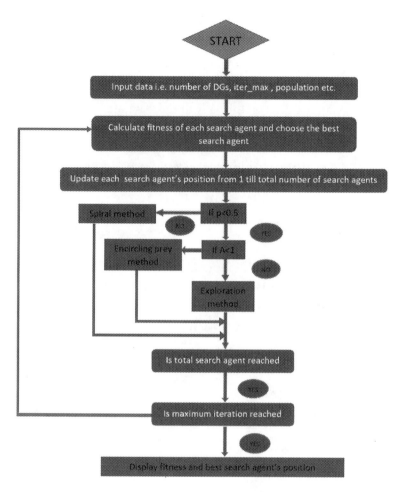

Figure 2-1. *Flowchart for the whale optimization algorithm*

Whale Pseudocode

The following pseudocode describes the whale optimization algorithm as outlined in Figure 2-1.

```
Randomly initialize the whale population.
Evaluate the fitness values of whales and find out the best
search agent X* .
```

```
Initialize the whales population Xi (i = 1, 2, ..., n)
Calculate the fitness of each search agent
X*=the best search agent
while (t < maximum number of iterations)
    for each search agent
    Update a, A, C, l, and p
        if1 (p<0.5)
            if2 (|A| < 1)
                Update the position of the current search agent
                by the Eq. (2.1)
            else if2 (|A|>=1)
                Select a random search agent ( )
                Update the position of the current search agent
                by the Eq. (2.3)
            end if2
        else if1 (p >=0.5)
                Update the position of the current search by
                the Eq. (2.3)
        end if1
    end for
    Check if any search agent goes beyond the search space and
    amend it
    Calculate the fitness of each search agent
    Update X* if there is a better solution
    t=t+1
end while
return X*
```

Whale Prerequisites and Code

Make sure that Java 8 (JDK8 or higher) is installed on your computer. An IDE like Eclipse is recommended but not necessary because you can use the command-line interface to run the code without an IDE.

The code for the whale algorithm contains the following classes.

- The Point utility class, with three members (see Listing 2-1)

  - A double array

  - An array of integers

  - An integer

- The Rastrigin utility class for the optimization evaluation function (see Listing 2-2 and Equation 2-5)

- The WhaleOptimizer optimization class, the main Java class for the functionality of the algorithm (see Listing 2-3)

$$f(\mathbf{x}) = An + \sum_{i=1}^{n} \left[x_i^2 - A\cos(2\pi x_i) \right]$$
$$\text{where: } A = 10$$

Equation 2-5. *Rastrigin benchmark function*

Listing 2-1. The Point Class

```
public class Point {
    public double p[];
    public int ip[];
    public int dim;
```

```java
public Point(double p[]) {
    this.dim = p.length;
    this.p = p.clone();
}

public Point(int p[]) {
    this.dim = p.length;
    this.ip = p.clone();
}

public Point(int dim) {
    this.dim = dim;
    p = new double[dim];
}
/*
this method returns the square root of the sum of the
square of the members in the array of doubles
*/
public double norm(){
    double sum = 0;
    for (int i = 0; i < dim ; i ++) {
        sum += Math.pow(this.p[i], 2);
    }
    return Math.sqrt(sum);
}
/*
This method returns the square root of the distance between
2 points. Its calculated by taking sum of the square of the
distance between each element of the double array and then
doing a square root of it.
*/
```

```java
public double dist(Point b){
    double sum = 0;
    for (int i = 0; i < dim ; i ++) {
        sum += Math.pow(this.p[i]-b.p[i], 2);
    }
    return Math.sqrt(sum);
}
/*
This method adds the two Points by taking sum of the
individual elements of the double array of each Point
*/

public static Point add(Point a, Point b) throws Exception {
    if (a.dim != b.dim){
        throw new IllegalArgumentException("Adding points
        from different dimensions");
    }
    int dim  = a.dim;
    double cp[] = new double[dim];
    for (int i = 0; i < dim; i++){
        cp[i] = a.p[i] + b.p[i];
    }
    return new Point(cp);
}
/*
This method adds the two Points by taking sum of the
individual elements of the double array of each Point and
then takes an average of each added elements and finally
returns a Point with the averages points in the new array
*/
```

```
public static Point mid(Point a, Point b) throws Exception{
    if (a.dim != b.dim){
        throw new IllegalArgumentException("Incompatible
        points");
    }
    int dim  = a.dim;
    double cor[] = new double[dim];
    for (int i = 0; i < dim; i++){
        cor[i] = (a.p[i] + b.p[i]) / 2.0;
    }
    return new Point (cor);
}
/*
This method multiplies each element of the array of double
with the constant a. a is the coefficient we use in the
optimization algorithm.
*/
public Point mull(double a) {
    double p[] = new double[this.dim];
    Point m = new Point(p);
    for (int i = 0; i < this.dim; i++){
        m.p[i] = this.p[i]*a;
    }
    return m;
}
/*
This method returns a string representation of the double
array
*/
```

```java
    @Override
    public String toString() {
        if (p != null) {
            String s = "[";
            for (int i = 0; i < this.dim; i++){
                s += (float)p[i];
                if (i == this.dim - 1) {
                    s += "]";
                } else {
                    s += ",";
                }
            }
            return s;
        } else {
            String s = "[";
            for (int i = 0; i < this.dim; i++){
                s += (int)ip[i];
                if (i == this.dim - 1) {
                    s += "]";
                } else {
                    s += ",";
                }
            }
            return s;
        }
    }
}
```

Listing 2-2. The Rastrigin Class

```
/*
This class is used as the benchmark function and will be
used throughout all algorithms.

*/
public class Rastrigin {

    private double A;
    private double n;

    public Rastrigin(double A, double n) {
        this.A = A;
        this.n = n;
    }

    /*
    This method is the main method for the Rastrigin benchmark
    function. It takes as input a Point object (explained
    above) and performs the calculations for the benchmark.
    */

    public double f(Point x) {
        double sum = 0;
        //o = numpy.sum(x ** 2 - 10 * numpy.cos(2 * math.pi *
            x)) + 10 * dim
        for (int i = 0; i < x.dim; i++) {

            sum += Math.pow(x.p[i], 2) - A*Math.cos(2*Math.
            PI*x.p[i]);

        }
        return A*n + sum;
    }
}
```

```
/*
```

This class is the main optimizer class. Our objective function is the minimization of the benchmark function (Rastrigin in this case)

Listing 2-3. The WhaleOptimizer Class

```
import java.lang.Math;
import java.util.*;
public class WhaleOptimizer
{
// declare variables for population size, number of iterations,
    dimensions and bounds.

int popSize;
int iterations;

int dimensions;
int ub=100,lb=-100;
// an array to represent the fitness values.
double fitness[];
// Represents the best Solution
double[] bestSolution;

double minValueOfSolution;
double leaderDistance;
double[][] positions;
// other constants used within the algorithm
double a,t,a2,p;

/*
Initialize the variables and arrays within the constructor.
We will initialize the population here with dimensions capped
between lower and upper bounds.
*/
```

```
public WhaleOptimizer(int iterations,int popSize, int
dimensions)
{
    this.iterations=iterations;
    this.popSize=popSize;
    this.dimensions=dimensions;
    positions=new double[popSize][dimensions];
    fitness=new double[popSize];
//Initialize the population of all solutions
    for(int i=0;i<popSize;i++)
    {
    for (int j=0;j<dimensions;j++)
    {
// cap the values between upper and lower bounds
        positions[i][j]=Math.random()*(ub-lb)+lb;
    }
    }
// calculate the fitness of each solution in the population
    for(int i=0;i<popSize;i++)
    {
        fitness[i]=fitnessCalculator(positions[i]);

    }
// Get the best solution in population with random initialized
    values.
    int bestIndex= indexOfSmallest(fitness);
    bestSolution=positions[bestIndex];
    minValueOfSolution=smallestInArray(fitness);
}
//rastrigin function used for calculating the fitness of the
solutions
```

```java
private  double fitnessCalculator(double[] candidate)
{

    Point p= new Point(candidate);
    Rastrigin rast=new Rastrigin(10,dimensions);
// The other benchmark which can be experimented with is Ackley.
    //Ackley ack=new Ackley(10,10,10,10);
    return rast.f(p);

}
/*
Helper method which finds the smallest member in an array of
doubles
*/
private static double smallestInArray(double[] array){

    // add this
    if (array.length == 0)
       return -1;

    int index = 0;
    double min = array[index];

    for (int i = 1; i < array.length; i++){
       if (array[i] <= min){
       min = array[i];
       //index = i;
       }
    }
    return min;
}
/*
Helper method which finds the index of the smallest member in
an array of doubles
```

```
*/

private static int indexOfSmallest(double[] array){

    // add this
    if (array.length == 0)
        return -1;

    int index = 0;
    double min = array[index];

    for (int i = 1; i < array.length; i++){
        if (array[i] <= min){
        min = array[i];
        index = i;
        }
    }
    return index;
}

/*
Main method for running the algorithm
*/
private void optimize()
{
    //main loop for iterating over configured number of
    iterations

    for(int i=0;i<iterations;i++){
        //loop over individual whale in the population. Each
        whale represents a solution in the
        //search space
        for(int j=0;j<popSize;j++)
        {
```

```
        //get positions of whales in bounds
        positions[j]=simpleBounds(positions[j],lb,ub);
        //System.out.println("velocities="+s[j][0]);

        // calculate fitness of each whale
                double fNew = fitnessCalculator(positions[j]);

         // Update the current best solution
      if (fNew < minValueOfSolution)
        {
         bestSolution =positions[j].clone();
         minValueOfSolution = fNew;

        }

     }
//loop over the population again
    for(int j=0;j<popSize;j++)
    {

     a = 2 - i * ((2) / iterations);
    // a decreases linearly from 2 to 0

    // a2 linearly decreases from -1 to -2 to calculate t
    a2 = -1 + i * ((-1) / iterations);
     double r1=Math.random();
     double r2=Math.random();
     //exploit phase starts

     double A = 2 * a * r1 - a;   // Equation 2.2 for
     calculating A
     double  C = 2 * r2 ; // Equation 2.2 for calculating C

     int    b = 1;
       double l = (a2 - 1) * Math.random() + 1;
```

```
//random variable for calculating probablity
p= Math.random();
// Iterate over individual dimension of each of the
   solution
for(int k=0;k<dimensions;k++)
{
    //check for probability value via a random variable p
//update position of individual whale using Equation 2.3

    if (p < 0.5)
    {
        if (Math.abs(A) >= 1)
            {
            int rand_leader_index = (int)Math.
            floor(popSize * Math.random());
            double[] X_rand = positions[rand_leader_
            index].clone();
    double val= C * X_rand[k] - positions[j][k];
            double D_X_rand = Math.abs(val);
      //update the whale position
      positions[j][k]= X_rand[k] - A * D_X_rand;

            }

            else if (Math.abs(A) < 1){
                double val=C * bestSolution[j] -
                positions[j][k];
            leaderDistance = Math.abs(val);
      //update the whale position
            positions[j][k] = bestSolution[j] - A *
            leaderDistance;
            }
    }
```

```
        else if (p >= 0.5)
        {

            double distance2Leader = Math.
            abs(bestSolution[j] - positions[j][k]);
        //update the whale position
        positions[j][k] = distance2Leader * Math.exp
        (b * l) * Math.cos(l * 2 * Math.PI)+
        bestSolution[j];

        }

    }
    }
            // print the best solution
    System.out.println("iter="+i+" best fitness is
    ="+minValueOfSolution);

    }

}

/*
Method for bounding the value between lower and upper bounds
*/
private double[] simpleBounds(double[] val, double lower,
double upper){
    double[] result = new double[val.length];
    for (int i = 0; i < val.length; i++) {

        if (val[i] < lower){
            result[i] = lower;
        }
```

```
      else if (val[i] > upper){
        result[i] = upper;
      }
      else
      {
          result[i]=val[i];
      }

  }
      return result;
}
/*
Main method to pass inputs and launch the algorithm
*/

public static void main(String[] args)
{
//takes input as number of iterations, population size and
dimensions
int iter=Integer.parseInt(args[0]);
int pop=Integer.parseInt(args[1]);
int dim=Integer.parseInt(args[2]);
WhaleOptimizer whale =new WhaleOptimizer(iter,pop,dim);
whale.optimize();
}

}
```

Executing the Whale Code

To compile the Java files, please use the following commands.

```
javac Point.java
javac Rastrigin.java
javac WhaleOptimizer.java
//running the example with 50 iterations and population size of
10 and 30 dimensions
java WhaleOptimizer 50 10 30
```

The following is the output of running the preceding code.

```
iter=0 best fitness is =64618.62705831786
iter=1 best fitness is =6089.687035911165
iter=2 best fitness is =1191.832252196124
iter=3 best fitness is =1191.832252196124
iter=4 best fitness is =557.1033568751382
iter=5 best fitness is =294.5584859459394
iter=6 best fitness is =227.37519747187895
iter=7 best fitness is =227.37519747187895
iter=8 best fitness is =169.87626519543952
iter=9 best fitness is =164.24808671529178
iter=10 best fitness is =164.24808671529178
iter=11 best fitness is =164.24808671529178
iter=12 best fitness is =38.5966387729996
iter=13 best fitness is =38.5966387729996
iter=14 best fitness is =38.5966387729996
iter=15 best fitness is =38.5966387729996
iter=16 best fitness is =38.5966387729996
iter=17 best fitness is =36.691018990274586
iter=18 best fitness is =31.104006893451526
iter=19 best fitness is =31.104006893451526
```

```
iter=20 best fitness is =31.104006893451526
iter=21 best fitness is =31.104006893451526
iter=22 best fitness is =31.104006893451526
iter=23 best fitness is =31.104006893451526
iter=24 best fitness is =31.104006893451526
iter=25 best fitness is =31.104006893451526
iter=26 best fitness is =31.104006893451526
iter=27 best fitness is =30.71055488621937
iter=28 best fitness is =30.030588201965543
iter=29 best fitness is =30.030588201965543
iter=30 best fitness is =30.030588201965543
iter=31 best fitness is =30.030588201965543
iter=32 best fitness is =30.01029093772968
iter=33 best fitness is =29.990401804857754
iter=34 best fitness is =29.990401804857754
iter=35 best fitness is =29.950989401883703
iter=36 best fitness is =29.950989401883703
iter=37 best fitness is =29.88823708275629
iter=38 best fitness is =29.883783242305753
iter=39 best fitness is =22.450413721771895
iter=40 best fitness is =5.573548743084075
iter=41 best fitness is =1.2819795525663835
iter=42 best fitness is =1.2819795525663835
iter=43 best fitness is =1.2819795525663835
iter=44 best fitness is =1.2819795525663835
iter=45 best fitness is =1.2819795525663835
iter=46 best fitness is =1.2819795525663835
iter=47 best fitness is =1.2819795525663835
iter=48 best fitness is =1.2819795525663835
iter=49 best fitness is =0.9079497282054376
```

History: Gray Wolves

A man might befriend a wolf, even break a wolf, but no man could truly tame a wolf.

—George R. R. Martin

This metaheuristic algorithm was proposed by Seyedali Mirajaliali, Seyed Muhammad, and Andrew Lewis in a 2014 paper. It was inspired by the social hierarchy in the hunting techniques of gray wolves.

The gray wolf social hierarchy is defined at four levels based on fitness.

- Level 1 (alpha)

  - The leader of the pack (can be male or female)

  - Responsible for making decisions such as when and where to hunt

  - Lower-level wolves follow the alpha and acknowledge it by holding their tails down

- Level 2 (beta)

  - These wolves assist the alpha in decision-making

  - Advises the alpha wolf and is responsible for maintaining discipline

  - Elects the alpha among themselves whenever needed (due to illness or death of former alpha)

  - Acts as the intermediary between the alpha and other lower wolves, sees that the orders of alpha are followed, and provides feedback to alpha

- Level 3 (delta)

  - They are called *subordinates*

  - Reports to alpha and beta and superior to omega

- • Deltas are further divided into

  - • Scouts who are responsible for keeping an eye on boundaries

  - • Sentinels responsible for protecting the pack

  - • Elders who are former alphas and betas

  - • Hunters who help alpha and beta with hunting

  - • Caretakers who help the ill and wounded in the pack

- • Level 4 (omega)

  - • Lowest in the hierarchy

  - • Mostly the scapegoat of the pack

  - • Must eat last in the pack

This hierarchy is illustrated in Figure 2-2.

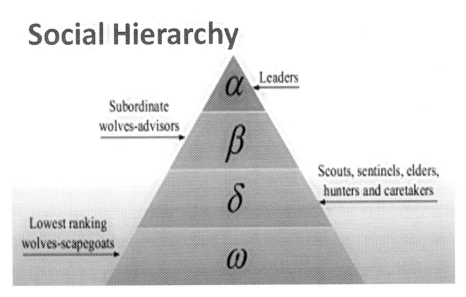

Figure 2-2. *The social hierarchy of gray wolves*

The more fit a wolf is, the higher the category it is in. This means the alpha wolf is most fit, followed by betas, then deltas, and finally omegas.

How Gray Wolf Optimization Works

The search process for finding the optimal solution works on the gray wolf hunting behavior model, which has three stages.

1. Search for the prey.

2. Encircle the prey.

3. Attack the prey.

The first two stages are exploratory, and the last one is exploiting.

Searching (Exploration)

The exploration is based on searching for prey by directions from wolves α, β, and δ. The $C\alpha$ parameter whose value, if >1, indicates that exploration is occurring. The C_p parameter introduces randomness in the distance between wolves and prey. This stochasticity is important to avoid the solution getting trapped in local optima.

Encircling (Exploration)

During hunting, gray wolves encircle their prey, which is represented mathematically by Equation 2-6.

$$D = |C \cdot X_p(t) - A \cdot X(t)|$$

$$X(t+1) = X_p(t) - A \cdot D$$

Equation 2-6. *Distance update between wolves and prey*

In Equation 2-6, t represents the current iteration, and A and C are coefficient vectors. X_p is the position vector of the prey, and X is the position vector of the wolf. The A and C vectors are calculated in Equation 2-7 and linearly decrease over the iterations. r_1 and r_2 are random variables.

$$A = 2a \cdot r_1 \cdot a$$

$$C = 2 \cdot r_2$$

Equation 2-7. *Updating coefficients*

Attacking (Exploitation)

The alpha wolves lead the attack. Beta and delta wolves might participate from time to time. The best solutions are derived based on the position of the alpha, beta, and delta wolves.

The attacking behavior is shown in Figure 2-3. It also depicts the exploitation phase of the process. When the $C\alpha$ parameter decreases, it implies that the wolf is moving toward the prey. Conversely, if $C\alpha$ increases, then the wolf is moving away from the prey. When this parameter becomes less than 1, the wolf is attacking the prey.

Wolf ω keeps updating its position based on the positions of wolves α, β, and δ. Equation 2-8 reflects updates in its position.

$$X_{\omega 1}^{iter} = X_{\alpha}^{iter} - c_1 D_{\alpha}^{iter}, \; X_{\omega 2}^{iter} = X_{\beta}^{iter} - c_2 D_{\beta}^{iter}, \; X_{\omega 3}^{iter} = X_{\delta}^{iter} - c_3 D_{\delta}^{iter}$$

$$X_{\omega}^{iter+1} = \frac{X_{\omega 1}^{iter} + X_{\omega 2}^{iter} + X_{\omega 3}^{iter}}{3}$$

$$D_{\alpha}^{iter} = \left| c_{\alpha} X_{\alpha}^{iter} - X^{iter} \right|, \; D_{\beta}^{iter} = \left| c_{\beta} X_{\beta}^{iter} - X^{iter} \right|, \; D_{\delta}^{iter} = \left| c_{\delta} X_{\delta}^{iter} - X^{iter} \right|$$

Equation 2-8. *Position update for omega wolves based on the position of wolves α, β, and δ*

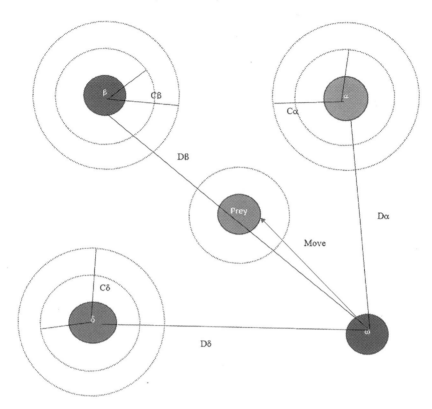

Figure 2-3. *Hunting behavior of gray wolves*

Gray Wolf Flowchart

Figure 2-4 illustrates the flowchart for the gray wolf optimization algorithm. At a high level, this flowchart starts by initializing parameters like the number of iterations and population size. During each iteration, the position of wolves is updated based on the location of the prey, and the fitness function of each wolf is calculated. After all the iterations, the best fitness value is chosen as the best solution.

Figure 2-4. *Gray wolf optimization flowchart*

Gray Wolves Pseudocode

The following pseudocode describes the gray wolf optimization algorithm as outlined in Figure 2-4.

```
Begin
Initialize the parameters popsize, maxiter, ub and lb where
popsize: size of population,
maxiter: maximum number of iterations,
ub: upper bound(s) of the variables,
lb: lower bound(s) of the variables;
Generate the initial positions of gray wolves with ub and lb;
Initialize and Calculate the fitness of each gray wolf;
alpha = the gray wolf with the first maximum fitness;
beta = the gray wolf with the second maximum fitness;
delta = the gray wolf with the third maximum fitness;
While
   for : popsize
     Update the position of the current gray wolf  ;
   end for
   Update and
   Calculate the fitness of all gray wolves;
   Update alpha, beta, and delta;
   ;
end while
Return alpha;
End
```

Gray Wolves Prerequisites and Code

Again, make sure that Java 8 (JDK8 or higher) is installed on your computer. An IDE like Eclipse is recommended but not necessary because you can use the command-line interface to run the code without an IDE.

The code for the whale algorithm contains the following Java classes.

- The Point utility class, with three members (see Listing 2-4)

  - A double array

  - An array of integers

  - An integer

- The Rastrigin utility class for the optimization evaluation function (see Listing 2-5 and Equation 2-9)

- The GrayWolfOptimizer optimization class, the main Java class for the functionality of the algorithm (see Listing 2-6)

$$f(\mathbf{x}) = An + \sum_{i=1}^{n} \left[x_i^2 - A\cos(2\pi x_i) \right]$$
$$\text{where: } A = 10$$

Equation 2-9. *Rastrigin benchmark function*

Listing 2-4. The Point Class

```java
public class Point {
    public double p[];
    public int ip[];
    public int dim;
```

```java
public Point(double p[]) {
    this.dim = p.length;
    this.p = p.clone();
}

public Point(int p[]) {
    this.dim = p.length;
    this.ip = p.clone();
}

public Point(int dim) {
    this.dim = dim;
    p = new double[dim];
}
/*
 this method returns the square root of the sum of the
 square of the members in the array of doubles
*/
public double norm(){
    double sum = 0;
    for (int i = 0; i < dim ; i ++) {
        sum += Math.pow(this.p[i], 2);
    }
    return Math.sqrt(sum);
}
/*
 This method returns the square root of the distance
 between 2 points. Its calculated by taking sum of the
 square of the distance between each element of the double
 array and then doing a square root of it.
*/
```

```java
public double dist(Point b){
    double sum = 0;
    for (int i = 0; i < dim ; i ++) {
        sum += Math.pow(this.p[i]-b.p[i], 2);
    }
    return Math.sqrt(sum);
}
/*
 This method adds the two Points by taking sum of the
 individual elements of the double array of each Point
*/

public static Point add(Point a, Point b) throws Exception
{
    if (a.dim != b.dim){
        throw new IllegalArgumentException("Adding points
        from different dimensions");
    }
    int dim  = a.dim;
    double cp[] = new double[dim];
    for (int i = 0; i < dim; i++){
        cp[i] = a.p[i] + b.p[i];
    }
    return new Point(cp);
}
 /*
This method adds the two Points by taking sum of the
individual elements of the double array of each Point and
then takes an average of each added elements and finally
returns a Point with the averages points in the new array
*/
```

```
public static Point mid(Point a, Point b) throws Exception{
    if (a.dim != b.dim){
        throw new IllegalArgumentException("Incompatible
        points");
    }
    int dim  = a.dim;
    double cor[] = new double[dim];
    for (int i = 0; i < dim; i++){
        cor[i] = (a.p[i] + b.p[i]) / 2.0;
    }
    return new Point (cor);
}
/*
This method multiplies each element of the array of double
with the constant a. a is the coefficient we use in the
optimization algorithm.
*/
public Point mull(double a) {
    double p[] = new double[this.dim];
    Point m = new Point(p);
    for (int i = 0; i < this.dim; i++){
        m.p[i] = this.p[i]*a;
    }
    return m;
}
/*
    This method returns a string representation of the
    double array
*/
```

```java
@Override
public String toString() {
    if (p != null) {
        String s = "[";
        for (int i = 0; i < this.dim; i++){
            s += (float)p[i];
            if (i == this.dim - 1) {
                s += "]";
            } else {
                s += ",";
            }
        }
        return s;
    } else {
        String s = "[";
        for (int i = 0; i < this.dim; i++){
            s += (int)ip[i];
            if (i == this.dim - 1) {
                s += "]";
            } else {
                s += ",";
            }
        }
        return s;
    }
}
```

Listing 2-5. The Rastrigin Class

```
    /*
    This class is used as the benchmark function and will be
    used throughout all algorithms.

    */

public class Rastrigin {

    private double A;
    private double n;

    public Rastrigin(double A, double n) {
        this.A = A;
        this.n = n;
    }

    /*
      This method is the main method for the Rastrigin benchmark
      function. It takes as input a Point object (explained
      above) and performs the calculations for the benchmark.
    */

    public double f(Point x) {
        double sum = 0;
        //o = numpy.sum(x ** 2 - 10 * numpy.cos(2 * math.pi *
        x)) + 10 * dim
        for (int i = 0; i < x.dim; i++) {

            sum += Math.pow(x.p[i], 2) - A*Math.cos(2*Math.
            PI*x.p[i]);

        }
        return A*n + sum;
    }

}
```

Listing 2-6. The GrayWolfOptimizer Class

```
/*
Main optimizer class for Gray Wolf optimization. Objective
function is minimizing the Rastrigin benchmark function
*/
import java.lang.Math;
import java.util.*;
public class GrayWolfOptimizer
{
// declare variables for population size, iterations and dimensions
int popSize;
int iterations;

int dimensions;
//declare upper and lower bounds for the search space
double ub=5.12,lb=-5.12;
//declare array for holding the fitness values
double fitness[];
// array which holds dimensions of the best solution
double[] bestSolution;
// declare coefficients like alpha, beta and gamma
double alpha = 0.5 ; // Randomness 0--1 (highly random)
double betamin = 0.20 ; // minimum value of beta
// minimum value of the solution
double minValueOfSolution;
//declare two dimensional array for holding position of each solution
double[][] positions;
double[][] positions1;
int[] sortedIndex;
double[] alphaPosition;
double[] betaPosition;
double[] deltaPosition;
```

```java
//start with a high value (randomly chosen as 100000000)
double alphaScore=10000000;
double betaScore=10000000;
double deltaScore=10000000;
public GrayWolfOptimizer(int iterations,int popSize, int
dimensions)
{
//initialize the iterations , population size and dimensions
    this.iterations=iterations;
    this.popSize=popSize;
    this.dimensions=dimensions;
    positions=new double[popSize][dimensions];
    positions1=new double[popSize][dimensions];

    fitness=new double[popSize];
    alphaPosition=new double[dimensions];
    betaPosition=new double[dimensions];
    deltaPosition=new double[dimensions];
    //loop through the population size and initialize the
      dimensions for each solution
    // in the population
    for(int i=0;i<popSize;i++)
    {

    for (int j=0;j<dimensions;j++)
    {
    // cap the positions between lower and upper bounds
        positions[i][j]=Math.random()*(ub-lb)+lb;

    }
    }

}
```

```
//rastrigin function used
private  double fitnessCalculator(double[] candidate)
{

    Point p= new Point(candidate);
    Rastrigin rast=new Rastrigin(10,dimensions);
    //Ackley ack=new Ackley(10,10,10,10);
    return rast.f(p);

}

/*
Method for updating the position of the wolves. This takes in a
coefficient as the parameter value
*/
private void updateWolvesPosition(double a)
{

    // Update the Position of search agents including omegas
        for (int i=0;i<popSize;i++)
        {
          for (int j=0;j<dimensions;j++){

                double r1 = Math.random()  ;// r1 is a random
                                              number in [0,1]
                double r2 = Math.random() ;//  r2 is a random
                                              number in [0,1]
// calculate A1 and C1 based on Equation 2-6.
                double A1 = 2 * a * r1 - a;
                double C1 = 2 * r2;
// update the position of alpha wolves
                double  D_alpha = Math.abs(C1 * alphaPosition[j] -
                positions[i][j]);
                double X1 = alphaPosition[j] - A1 * D_alpha;
```

```
            r1 = Math.random()   ;// r1 is a random number in
                                   [0,1]
            r2 = Math.random() ;//  r2 is a random number in
                                   [0,1]

            double A2 = 2 * a * r1 - a;
            double C2 = 2 * r2;
// update the position of beta wolves

            double D_beta = Math.abs(C2 * betaPosition[j] -
            positions[i][j]);
            double X2 = betaPosition[j] - A2 * D_beta;

            r1 = Math.random();
            r2 = Math.random();

            double A3 = 2 * a * r1 - a;
            double C3 = 2 * r2;
// update the position of delta wolves

            double D_delta = Math.abs(C3 * deltaPosition[j] -
            positions[i][j]);
            double X3 = deltaPosition[j] - A3 * D_delta;

            positions[i][j] = (X1 + X2 + X3) / 3  ;
            // Equation (2.8)
                }

        }
}
/*
This code is main method for the Gray Wolf optimization
algorithm
*/
```

```
private void optimize()
{

    //main loop for number of iterations
    for(int it=0;it<iterations;it++){
        //loop over individual

    // loop through individual solution (wolves) in each iteration
        for(int i=0;i<popSize;i++)
    {
                        // calculate fitness of each solution
        fitness[i]=fitnessCalculator(positions[i]);

        // Update Alpha, Beta, and Delta scores and positions
          of alpha, beta and delta wolves
          if (fitness[i] < alphaScore)
            {
              deltaScore=betaScore;
                 deltaPosition=betaPosition.clone();
              betaScore=alphaScore;
              betaPosition=alphaPosition.clone();
              alphaScore=fitness[i];
              alphaPosition=positions[i].clone();
            }
        // Update Alpha, Beta, and Delta scores and positions
          of alpha, beta and delta wolves

            if (fitness[i] > alphaScore && fitness[i] <
            betaScore)
            {
            deltaScore=betaScore;
               deltaPosition=betaPosition.clone();
            betaScore=fitness[i];
```

```
            betaPosition=positions[i].clone();
            }

        // Update Alpha, Beta, and Delta scores and positions
            of alpha, beta and delta wolves

        if (fitness[i] > alphaScore && fitness[i] > betaScore
        && fitness[i] < deltaScore)
        {
            deltaScore = fitness[i] ;
            deltaPosition=positions[i].clone();

        }

         double a = 2 - it * ((2) / iterations);
        // in each iteration update positions of wolves based
            on updates to a
updateWolvesPosition(a);
            }

    System.out.println("best score after iteration "+it+"
    ="+alphaScore);
}
}
/*
Main method for executing the code. It takes as input the
number of iterations, population Size and number of dimensions
as command line parameters
*/
public static void main(String[] args)
{
int iter=Integer.parseInt(args[0]);
int pop=Integer.parseInt(args[1]);
int dim=Integer.parseInt(args[2]);
```

```
GrayWolfOptimizer gwo =new GrayWolfOptimizer(iter,pop,dim);
gwo.optimize();
}
}
```

Executing the Wolf Code

The following code compiles the files.

```
javac Point.java
javac Rastrigin.java
javac GrayWolfOptimizer.java

//running the example with 50 iterations and population size of
10 and 30 dimensions
java GrayWolfOptimizer 50 10 30
```

The following is the output of running the preceding code.

```
best score after iteration 0 =509.96673667327343
best score after iteration 1 =426.41598649085057
best score after iteration 2 =338.22309610465413
best score after iteration 3 =308.52361359264995
best score after iteration 4 =277.9213584359936
best score after iteration 5 =248.83646851559863
best score after iteration 6 =203.07265223211158
best score after iteration 7 =203.07265223211158
best score after iteration 8 =203.07265223211158
best score after iteration 9 =203.07265223211158
best score after iteration 10 =203.07265223211158
best score after iteration 11 =203.07265223211158
best score after iteration 12 =203.07265223211158
best score after iteration 13 =184.70404858170573
```

```
best score after iteration 14 =184.70404858170573
best score after iteration 15 =184.70404858170573
best score after iteration 16 =184.70404858170573
best score after iteration 17 =184.70404858170573
best score after iteration 18 =184.70404858170573
best score after iteration 19 =182.58434165600903
best score after iteration 20 =182.58434165600903
best score after iteration 21 =181.7495365991856
best score after iteration 22 =181.7495365991856
best score after iteration 23 =181.663022402521
best score after iteration 24 =181.663022402521
best score after iteration 25 =157.10334848914758
best score after iteration 26 =156.35153795887368
best score after iteration 27 =139.32771778897705
best score after iteration 28 =139.32771778897705
best score after iteration 29 =139.32771778897705
best score after iteration 30 =137.75584129668897
best score after iteration 31 =137.75584129668897
best score after iteration 32 =137.75584129668897
best score after iteration 33 =128.32651340584417
best score after iteration 34 =126.37388487653246
best score after iteration 35 =126.37388487653246
best score after iteration 36 =126.37388487653246
best score after iteration 37 =126.37388487653246
best score after iteration 38 =124.71241252923625
best score after iteration 39 =124.71241252923625
best score after iteration 40 =124.71241252923625
best score after iteration 41 =124.71241252923625
best score after iteration 42 =124.71241252923625
best score after iteration 43 =124.71241252923625
best score after iteration 44 =124.71241252923625
```

```
best score after iteration 45 =124.71241252923625
best score after iteration 46 =124.71241252923625
best score after iteration 47 =124.71241252923625
best score after iteration 48 =124.71241252923625
best score after iteration 49 =124.71241252923625
```

History: Bats

Bumblebee bat, how do you see at night?

I make a squeaky sound that bounces back from whatever it hits. I see by hearing.

— *Darrin Lunde*

The bat algorithm is in line with the other metaheuristic algorithms, which approximate NP-hard problems. Xin-She Yang developed the algorithm in 2010.

This algorithm is based on the echolocation capabilities of microbats, where the rate of emission and loudness are varied.

A microbat is a tiny bat weighing around 2 grams. Echolocation is the sound pulse emitted by the bats at a definite angle. A bat listens to the echo of that sound wave after it bounces back from surrounding objects. This helps the bat to locate prey and avoid obstacles. The frequency of the sound waves ranges from 25 kHz to 150 kHz.

Figure 2-5 illustrates how echolocation works as a bat emits sonar waves. The distance from an obstacle is calculated by combining the time it takes a soundwave to bounce back and the frequency of the emitted wave.

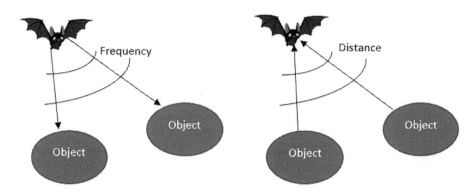

Figure 2-5. *Echolocation in bats*

Bats use the dimensions shown in Figure 2-6 to search for prey.

Figure 2-6. *Various dimensions for bats*

Bats automatically adjust the frequency or wavelength of the emitted pulses based on how far they are from their prey. The assumption is that loudness varies from a very high value ($A0$) to a fixed minimum value. Equation 2-10 calculates a bat's changing position and velocity.

$$f_i = f_{\min} + (f_{\max} - f_{\min})\beta,$$

$$v_i^t = v_i^{t-1} + (x_i^{t-1} - x_*)f_i,$$

$$x_i^t = x_i^{t-1} + v_i^t,$$

$$A_i^{t+1} = \alpha A_i^t, \quad r_i^{t+1} = r_i^0[1 - \exp(-\gamma t)],$$

$$A_i^t \to 0, \quad r_i^t \to r_i^0, \text{ as } t \to \infty.$$

Equation 2-10. *Changing location and velocity based on the position of an object*

Bat Flowchart

Figure 2-7 is the flowchart for the bat optimization algorithm. At a high level, this flowchart starts by initializing the parameters (e.g., the number of iterations and bat population size). During each iteration, the bats' location and velocity are updated, and the fitness function of each bat is calculated. After all the iterations, the best fitness value is chosen as the best solution.

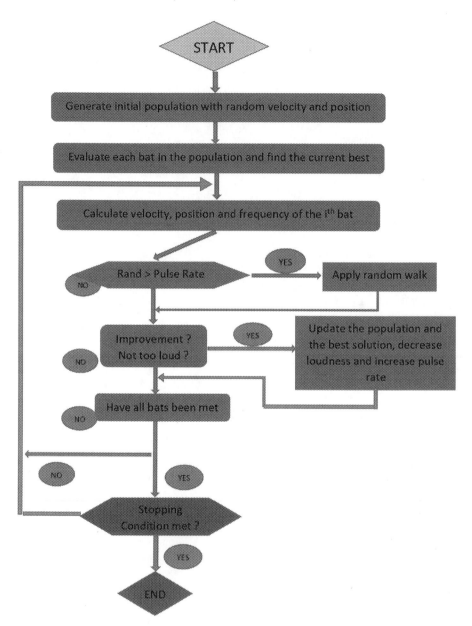

Figure 2-7. *Bat optimization flowchart*

Bats Pseudocode

The following pseudocode describes the bat optimization algorithm as outlined in Figure 2-7.

```
Objective function f(x), x = (x1, ..., xd)
Initialize the bat population Xi (i = 1, 2, . . ., n)
Define the pulse rate ri and the loudness Ai
Input: Initial bat population
while ( t < Max number of iterations ) do
    Generate new solutions by adjusting frequency, and
    updating velocities and locations/solutions (Equations
    in 2-10 )
    if ( rand > ri ) then
            Select a solution among the best solutions
            Generate a local solution around the selected best
            solution
    end if
    Generate a new solution by flying randomly
    if ( rand < Ai & f(Xi) < f(X*) ) then
            Accept the new solutions
            Increase emission rate and reduce loudness
    end if
    Rank the bats and find the current best Xbest
end while
Output: Best bat found (i.e. best solution)
```

Bats Prerequisites and Bat Code

Once more, make sure that Java 8 (JDK8 or higher) is installed on your computer. An IDE like Eclipse is recommended but not necessary because you can use the command-line interface to run the code without an IDE.

The code for the bat algorithm contains the following classes.

- The Point utility class, with three members
  (see Listing 2-7)

  - A double array

  - An array of integers

  - An integer

- The Rastrigin utility class for the optimization
  evaluation function (see Listing 2-8 and Equation 2-11)

- The BatOptimizer optimization class, the main
  Java class for the functionality of the algorithm
  (see Listing 2-9)

$$f(\mathbf{x}) = An + \sum_{i=1}^{n} \left[x_i^2 - A\cos(2\pi x_i) \right]$$
$$\text{where: } A = 10$$

Equation 2-11. *Rastrigin benchmark function*

Listing 2-7. The Point Class

```
public class Point {
    public double p[];
    public int ip[];
    public int dim;

    public Point(double p[]) {
        this.dim = p.length;
        this.p = p.clone();
    }
}
```

```java
public Point(int p[]) {
    this.dim = p.length;
    this.ip = p.clone();
}

public Point(int dim) {
    this.dim = dim;
    p = new double[dim];
}
 /*
 this method returns the square root of the sum of the
 square of the members in the array of doubles
 */
public double norm(){
    double sum = 0;
    for (int i = 0; i < dim ; i ++) {
        sum += Math.pow(this.p[i], 2);
    }
    return Math.sqrt(sum);
}
/*
  This method returns the square root of the distance
  between 2 points. Its calculated by taking sum of the
  square of the distance between each element of the double
  array and then doing a square root of it.
*/
public double dist(Point b){
    double sum = 0;
    for (int i = 0; i < dim ; i ++) {
        sum += Math.pow(this.p[i]-b.p[i], 2);
    }
```

```
        return Math.sqrt(sum);
    }
    /*
      This method adds the two Points by taking sum of the
      individual elements of the double array of each Point
     */

    public static Point add(Point a, Point b) throws Exception {
        if (a.dim != b.dim){
            throw new IllegalArgumentException("Adding points
            from different dimensions");
        }
        int dim  = a.dim;
        double cp[] = new double[dim];
        for (int i = 0; i < dim; i++){
            cp[i] = a.p[i] + b.p[i];
        }
        return new Point(cp);
    }
    /*
      This method adds the two Points by taking sum of the
      individual elements of the double array of each Point
      and then takes an average of each added elements and
      finally returns a Point with the averages points in the
      new array
     */

    public static Point mid(Point a, Point b) throws Exception{
        if (a.dim != b.dim){
            throw new IllegalArgumentException("Incompatible
            points");
        }
```

```
    int dim  = a.dim;
    double cor[] = new double[dim];
    for (int i = 0; i < dim; i++){
        cor[i] = (a.p[i] + b.p[i]) / 2.0;
    }
    return new Point (cor);
}
/*
  This method multiplies each element of the array of
  double with the constant a. a is the coefficient we use
  in the optimization algorithm.
 */
public Point mull(double a) {
    double p[] = new double[this.dim];
    Point m = new Point(p);
    for (int i = 0; i < this.dim; i++){
        m.p[i] = this.p[i]*a;
    }
    return m;
}
/*
   This method returns a string representation of the
   double array
  */

@Override
public String toString() {
    if (p != null) {
        String s = "[";
        for (int i = 0; i < this.dim; i++){
            s += (float)p[i];
```

```
                if (i == this.dim - 1) {
                    s += "]";
                } else {
                    s += ",";
                }
            }
            return s;
        } else {
            String s = "[";
            for (int i = 0; i < this.dim; i++){
                s += (int)ip[i];
                if (i == this.dim - 1) {
                    s += "]";
                } else {
                    s += ",";
                }
            }
            return s;
        }
    }
}
```

Listing 2-8. The Rastrigin Class

```
/*
This class is used as the benchmark function and will be
used throughout all algorithms.

*/
```

```java
public class Rastrigin {

    private double A;
    private double n;

    public Rastrigin(double A, double n) {
        this.A = A;
        this.n = n;
    }

    /*
      This method is the main method for the Rastrigin
      benchmark function. It takes as input a Point object
      (explained above) and performs the calculations for the
      benchmark.
      */

    public double f(Point x) {
        double sum = 0;
        //o = numpy.sum(x ** 2 - 10 * numpy.cos
        (2 * math.pi * x)) + 10 * dim
        for (int i = 0; i < x.dim; i++) {

            sum += Math.pow(x.p[i], 2) - A*Math.cos(2*Math.
            PI*x.p[i]);

        }
        return A*n + sum;
    }

}
```

Listing 2-9. The BatOptimizer Class

```
/*
Main class for the Bat optimizer. Goal is to minimize the
objective function represented by the Rastrigin benchmark
*/
import java.lang.Math;
import java.util.*;
public class BatOptimizer
{
// Declare number of iterations, population size and dimensions
of each bat
int popSize;
int iterations;
int dimensions;
int ub=100,lb=-100;
// declare different coefficients and constants for the algo
double a=0.5;
double r=0.5;
double freq_min=0;
double freq_max=2;
// double array to hold the frequencies
double[] frequencies;
//two dimensional array of doubles for bat velocities
double[][] velocities;
double[][] solutions;
// array holding fitness value for each solution
double fitness[];
double[] bestSolution;
double[][] s;
double minValueOfSolution;
```

```
/*
Constructor for initializing the population and populating
initial fitness of each solution (bat)
*/
public BatOptimizer(int iterations,int popSize, int dimensions)
{
    this.iterations=iterations;
    this.popSize=popSize;
    this.dimensions=dimensions;
    frequencies=new double[popSize];
    velocities=new double[popSize][dimensions];
    solutions=new double[popSize][dimensions];
    s=new double[popSize][dimensions];
    fitness=new double[popSize];
    //initialize solutions by looping over each member in the
    population

    for(int i=0;i<popSize;i++)
    {
    for (int j=0;j<dimensions;j++)
    {

        solutions[i][j]=Math.random()*(ub-lb)+lb;
    }
    }
    // calculate fitness of each solution
    for(int i=0;i<popSize;i++)
    {
        fitness[i]=fitnessCalculator(solutions[i]);
    }
```

```
// find the index of the best solution initially as well as the
   bestSolution
    int bestIndex= indexOfSmallest(fitness);
    bestSolution=solutions[bestIndex];
    minValueOfSolution=smallestInArray(fitness);
}
//rastrigin function used
private  double fitnessCalculator(double[] candidate)
{

    Point p= new Point(candidate);
    Rastrigin rast=new Rastrigin(10,dimensions);
    return rast.f(p);

    }
/*
Helper method for returning smallest value in array of doubles.
*/
private static double smallestInArray(double[] array){

    // add this
    if (array.length == 0)
       return -1;

    int index = 0;
    double min = array[index];

    for (int i = 1; i < array.length; i++){
       if (array[i] <= min){
       min = array[i];
       //index = i;
       }
    }
    return min;
}
```

```java
/*
Helper method for returning index of the smallest member in the
array
*/

private static int indexOfSmallest(double[] array){

    // add this
    if (array.length == 0)
        return -1;

    int index = 0;
    double min = array[index];

    for (int i = 1; i < array.length; i++){
        if (array[i] <= min){
        min = array[i];
        index = i;
        }
    }
    return index;
}
/*
Main method of the algorithm
*/

private void optimize()
{
    //main loop for number of iterations

    for(int i=0;i<iterations;i++){
        //loop over individual bat
```

```
for(int j=0;j<popSize;j++)
{
    // update frequency of each bat
    frequencies[j]=freq_min+(freq_max-freq_min)*Math.
    random();
    //velocities update for each bat

        //v[i, :] = v[i, :] + (Sol[i, :] - best) * Q[i]
// calculate difference from the best solution
double[] diffFromBest=subtractElementwise(solutions[j],
bestSolution,frequencies);
        //update velocities for the bat
        velocities[j]= addElementwise(velocities[j],
        diffFromBest);

        s[j]= addElementwise(solutions[j],
        velocities[j]);

        s[j]=simpleBounds(s[j],lb,ub);

    if( Math.random() > r){

        s[j] = addArrayToRnd(bestSolution , 0.001 * rnd
        (dimensions));

        }

        //update the solution if fitness is better for the
        candidate
        // Evaluate new solutions
```

```java
double fNew = fitnessCalculator(s[j]);

// Update if the solution improves
if ((fNew <= fitness[j]) && (Math.random() < a))
  {
      solutions[j]= s[j].clone();
   //Sol[i, :] = numpy.copy(S[i, :])
   fitness[j] = fNew;
  }

   // Update the current best solution
if (fNew <= minValueOfSolution)
  {
   bestSolution =s[j].clone();
   minValueOfSolution = fNew;

  }

  }
System.out.println("iter="+i+" best fitness is
="+minValueOfSolution);
  }

}
/*
Helper method for returning a new array of double by adding the
passed argument to individual member of the array
*/

private static double[] addArrayToRnd(double[] a, double num)
throws ArithmeticException {
```

```
        double[] result = new double[a.length];
        for (int i = 0; i < a.length; i++) {
            result[i] = (a[i] + num);
        }
        return result;
}
/*
Helper method for returning a random value sampled from a
gaussian
*/

private double rnd(int dim)
{
    Random r = new Random(dim);
double randomValue =  0+ r.nextGaussian()*1;
return randomValue;
}
/*
Helper method for keeping values in between lower and upper
bounds
*/
private double[] simpleBounds(double[] val, double lower,
double upper){
    double[] result = new double[val.length];
    for (int i = 0; i < val.length; i++) {

        if (val[i] < lower){
            result[i] = lower;
          }
```

```
    else if (val[i] > upper){
       result[i] = upper;
     }
     else
     {
         result[i]=val[i];
     }

  }

     return result;
}
/*
Helper method for returning difference between the elements
of two array of doubles multiplied by the frequency of the
specific bat
*/

 private static double[] subtractElementwise(double[] a,
double[] b, double[] freq) throws ArithmeticException {

       if (a.length != b.length) {
          throw new ArithmeticException();
       } else {
          double[] result = new double[a.length];
          for (int i = 0; i < a.length; i++) {
             result[i] = (a[i] - b[i])*freq[i];
          }
          return result;
       }

  }
```

```
/*
Helper method for adding individual elements of the arrays of
doubles
*/

private static double[] addElementwise(double[] a, double[] b)
throws ArithmeticException {

        if (a.length != b.length) {
            throw new ArithmeticException();
        } else {
            double[] result = new double[a.length];
            for (int i = 0; i < a.length; i++) {
                result[i] = (a[i] + b[i]);
            }
            return result;
        }

    }
public static void main(String[] args)
{
int iter=Integer.parseInt(args[0]);
int pop=Integer.parseInt(args[1]);
int dim=Integer.parseInt(args[2]);
BatOptimizer bat=new BatOptimizer(iter,pop,dim);
bat.optimize();
}

}
```

Executing the Bat Code

The following code compiles the files.

```
javac Point.java
javac Rastrigin.java
javac BatOptimizer.java

//running the example with 50 iterations and population size of
10 and 30 dimensions
java BatOptimizer 50 10 30
```

The following is the output from running the preceding code.

```
iter=0 best fitness is =76483.71345283325
iter=1 best fitness is =76478.96155973038
iter=2 best fitness is =42783.77839770218
iter=3 best fitness is =42781.20842991052
iter=4 best fitness is =42779.167603237656
iter=5 best fitness is =42776.63576280687
iter=6 best fitness is =42774.62583068019
iter=7 best fitness is =42772.62987212166
iter=8 best fitness is =42771.63717776008
iter=9 best fitness is =42769.66244601229
iter=10 best fitness is =42766.72724352279
iter=11 best fitness is =42764.3061741315
iter=12 best fitness is =42761.43117104229
iter=13 best fitness is =42758.589572619385
iter=14 best fitness is =42755.31708648613
iter=15 best fitness is =42753.00804487652
iter=16 best fitness is =42751.17802334106
iter=17 best fitness is =42748.01258167695
iter=18 best fitness is =42746.22509580061
iter=19 best fitness is =42743.57316308794
```

```
iter=20 best fitness is =42742.260442575454
iter=21 best fitness is =42741.82483808292
iter=22 best fitness is =42738.80326661441
iter=23 best fitness is =42736.25202522932
iter=24 best fitness is =42733.320918717385
iter=25 best fitness is =42731.25727358482
iter=26 best fitness is =42728.007604724946
iter=27 best fitness is =42726.406891353756
iter=28 best fitness is =42723.64438883426
iter=29 best fitness is =42721.315796905874
iter=30 best fitness is =42718.64490574986
iter=31 best fitness is =42716.767293101264
iter=32 best fitness is =42714.54728307373
iter=33 best fitness is =42713.45080389827
iter=34 best fitness is =42711.64333019462
iter=35 best fitness is =42709.50725503373
iter=36 best fitness is =42708.10307075944
iter=37 best fitness is =42707.40691961385
iter=38 best fitness is =42705.34214633038
iter=39 best fitness is =42704.66175678234
iter=40 best fitness is =42703.64852114836
iter=41 best fitness is =42702.31121228729
iter=42 best fitness is =42700.33439530883
iter=43 best fitness is =42698.713593464
iter=44 best fitness is =42697.752620941945
iter=45 best fitness is =42695.54366609986
iter=46 best fitness is =42693.68707677068
iter=47 best fitness is =42691.56348775477
iter=48 best fitness is =42690.37030417116
iter=49 best fitness is =42688.31731561078
```

Summary

This chapter introduced optimization problem solutions specific to mammals, particularly whales, gray wolves, and bats. It covered the basic flow of optimization problems and solutions and presented relevant flowcharts, pseudocode, and code written in Java. The Rastrigin benchmark function was used as the objective function for all the algorithms.

CHAPTER 3

Birds: Particle Swarm and Cuckoo Search Optimization

This chapter discusses how birds use flock behavior for foraging. In this process, they look for ways to optimize their food search. The chapter briefly covers the history of this behavior and then discusses the algorithms powering birds' search behavior.

History: Particle Swarm

Birds of a Feather Flock Together

Swarm behavior is a collective behavior exhibited by a group of entities—animals, birds, or insects—when involved in activities like foraging or migration. The collective of animals or birds moves in synchrony in a specific direction. From a more abstract notion, swarm behavior is a disciplined action based on principles of self-organization. There is no central leader of the flock. It is mostly decentralized and self-regulated behavior, with some random movements. An example of bird flocking is shown in Figure 3-1.

© Shashank Jain 2022
S. Jain, *Nature-Inspired Optimization Algorithms with Java*,
https://doi.org/10.1007/978-1-4842-7401-9_3

The birds follow three simple rules, as explained in Craig W. Reynolds's 1987 paper.

- **Collision avoidance**: Each bird avoids colliding with the other birds in the flock.

- **Velocity uniformity**: All birds keep the same velocity.

- **Flock centering**. All birds try to move toward the center of the flock.

Figure 3-1. *Bird flock*

In a bird swarm, there is a local behavior associated with each bird, called the *cognitive component*. There is also a global behavior called the *social component*. The dynamics of a swarm are based on the history of previous behaviors shown by an individual member and that of the entire group. The birds change their position and velocity based on their own experience and that of the group.

Particle Swarm Optimization (PSO) Algorithm

The population of N particles is assumed. Each particle here represents a solution in the search space. Each particle is supposed to have dimensions of size D (a vector representation per particle that encapsulates the distance and velocity of the particle). The objective function is defined based on the criteria specified for the specific problem. The population of particles is distributed uniformly across the search space. The velocities and locations are randomly assigned initially.

A global minimum must be located within a search space. This translates to finding the best solution in the space. There is only one global minimum. None of the particles know where the global minima are. All they know is the *fitness function* for each particle.

Particles move with certain velocities, which are selected randomly in each iteration. This allows them to explore the search space and constantly update their position. Each bird changes its location as it moves with a certain velocity. It tries to find food based on its intuition but is also influenced by the group's behavior. As particles move in the search space, they remember their best position and the group's best position, as shown in Equation 3-1. This always influences the particle to move in that direction and makes them speed up toward that direction.

Equation 3-1 first updates the velocity (V) and then the location (P) of the particle.

$$P_i^{t+1} = P_i^t + V_i^{t+1}$$

$$V_i^{t+1} = \underbrace{wV_i^t}_{\text{Inertia}} + \underbrace{c_1 r_1 \left(P_{best(i)}^t - P_i^t \right)}_{\text{Cognitive (Personal)}} + \underbrace{c_2 r_2 \left(P_{bestglobal}^t - P_i^t \right)}_{\text{Social (Global)}}$$

Equation 3-1. *Update velocity based on local best and global best positions*

The first equation in Equation 3-1 is the update to the location.

The second equation in Equation 3-1 is the update to the velocity at each timestamp. It has three terms.

- It is the inertia at the current time.

- The second term updates the velocity of a particle at time $t+1$ by subtracting the current particle position from the best position particle has seen for itself. This makes the particle move toward its best position.

- The third term makes the update of particle velocity move toward the global best position seen so far as a flock.

Once the update happens to the particle velocity at time $t+1$, the location is also updated at time $t+1$ using the first equation.

There are also two coefficients in the second equation: $c_1 r_1$ and $c_2 r_2$. These coefficients control the levels of exploration and exploitation. **Exploitation** is the ability of particles to target the best solutions found so far. **Exploration**, on the other hand, is the ability of particles to evaluate the entire research space. The challenge of the remaining part of the article is to determine the impact of these coefficients to find a good balance between exploration and exploitation.

PSO Algorithm Flowchart

The flowchart of the PSO algorithm is depicted in Figure 3-2. The algorithm initializes the population, the number of iterations, and other parameters. During each iteration, each particle's velocity is updated and then the location. During each iteration, the fitness of each particle is calculated, and a global and local best is estimated. This continues until the max iterations are reached and global maxima are obtained.

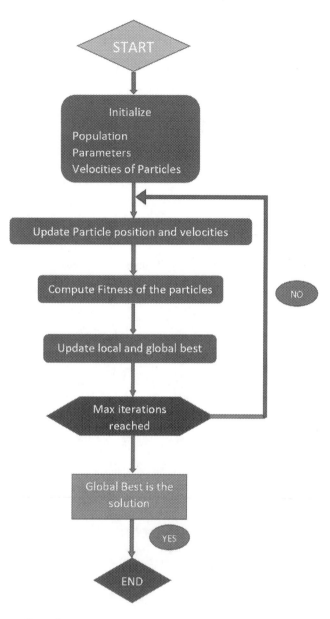

Figure 3-2. *Flowchart*

PSO Pseudocode

The following pseudocode describes the PSO algorithm as outlined in Figure 3-2.

```
For each particle
{
    Initialize particle
}

Do until maximum iterations are done
{
    For each particle
    {
        Calculate Data fitness value
        If the fitness value is better than pBest
        {
            Set pBest = current fitness value
        }
        If pBest is better than gBest
        {
            Set gBest = pBest
        }
    }

    For each particle
    {
        Calculate particle Velocity
        Use gBest and Velocity to update particle Data
    }
}
```

PSO Prerequisites and Code

Make sure that Java 8 (JDK8 or higher) is installed on your computer. An IDE like Eclipse is recommended but not necessary because you can use the command-line interface to run the code without an IDE.

The code for the PSO algorithm consists of two utility classes and an optimizer class.

- The Point utility class, with three members (see Listing 3-1)

  - A double array

  - An array of integers

  - An integer

- The Rastrigin utility class for the optimization evaluation function (see Listing 3-2)

- The ParticleSwarmOptimizer class, the main Java class for the algorithm's functionality (see Listing 3-3)

The Rastrigin benchmark function is shown in Equation 3-2.

$$f(\mathbf{x}) = An + \sum_{i=1}^{n} \left[x_i^2 - A\cos(2\pi x_i) \right]$$

$$\text{where: } A = 10$$

Equation 3-2. *Rastrigin benchmark function*

Listing 3-1. The Point Class

```java
public class Point {
    public double p[];
    public int ip[];
    public int dim;

    public Point(double p[]) {
        this.dim = p.length;
        this.p = p.clone();
    }

    public Point(int p[]) {
        this.dim = p.length;
        this.ip = p.clone();
    }

    public Point(int dim) {
        this.dim = dim;
        p = new double[dim];
    }
    /*
    this method returns the square root of the sum of the
    square of the members in the array of doubles
    */
    public double norm(){
        double sum = 0;
        for (int i = 0; i < dim ; i ++) {
            sum += Math.pow(this.p[i], 2);
        }
        return Math.sqrt(sum);
    }
```

```
/*
This method returns the square root of the distance between
2 points. It's calculated by taking sum of the square of
the distance between each element of the double array and
then doing a square root of it.
*/
public double dist(Point b){
    double sum = 0;
    for (int i = 0; i < dim ; i ++) {
        sum += Math.pow(this.p[i]-b.p[i], 2);
    }
    return Math.sqrt(sum);
}
/*
This method adds the two Points by taking sum of the
individual elements of the double array of each Point
*/

public static Point add(Point a, Point b) throws Exception
{
    if (a.dim != b.dim){
        throw new IllegalArgumentException("Adding points
        from different dimensions");
    }
    int dim  = a.dim;
    double cp[] = new double[dim];
    for (int i = 0; i < dim; i++){
        cp[i] = a.p[i] + b.p[i];
    }
    return new Point(cp);
}
```

```
/*
This method adds the two Points by taking sum of the
individual elements of the double array of each Point and
then takes an average of each added elements and finally
returns a Point with the averages points in the new array
*/

public static Point mid(Point a, Point b) throws Exception{
    if (a.dim != b.dim){
        throw new IllegalArgumentException
        ("Incompatible points");
    }
    int dim  = a.dim;
    double cor[] = new double[dim];
    for (int i = 0; i < dim; i++){
        cor[i] = (a.p[i] + b.p[i]) / 2.0;
    }
    return new Point (cor);
}
/*
 This method multiplies each element of the array of double
 with the constant a. a is the coefficient we use in the
 optimization algorithm.
*/
public Point mull(double a) {
    double p[] = new double[this.dim];
    Point m = new Point(p);
    for (int i = 0; i < this.dim; i++){
        m.p[i] = this.p[i]*a;
    }
    return m;
}
```

```
/*
This method returns a string representation of the double
array
 */

@Override
public String toString() {
    if (p != null) {
        String s = "[";
        for (int i = 0; i < this.dim; i++){
            s += (float)p[i];
            if (i == this.dim - 1) {
                s += "]";
            } else {
                s += ",";
            }
        }
        return s;
    } else {
        String s = "[";
        for (int i = 0; i < this.dim; i++){
            s += (int)ip[i];
            if (i == this.dim - 1) {
                s += "]";
            } else {
                s += ",";
            }
        }
        return s;
    }
}
}// Point class ends here.
```

Next is the next Java class, which is the Rastrigin class used as a benchmark function.

Listing 3-2. The Rastrigin Class

```
/*
This class is used as the benchmark function and will be
used throughout all algorithms.

*/
public class Rastrigin {

    private double A;
    private double n;

    public Rastrigin(double A, double n) {
        this.A = A;
        this.n = n;
    }

    /*
    This method is the main method for the Rastrigin benchmark
    function. It takes as input a Point object (explained above)
    and performs the calculations for the benchmark.
    */

    public double f(Point x) {
        double sum = 0;
        //o = numpy.sum(x ** 2 - 10 * numpy.cos(2 * math.pi *
        x)) + 10 * dim
        for (int i = 0; i < x.dim; i++) {

            sum += Math.pow(x.p[i], 2) - A*Math.cos(2*Math.
            PI*x.p[i]);

        }
```

```
        return A*n + sum;
    }

}//Rastrigin class ends here
```

Listing 3-3. The PSO Class

```
/*
Main class for the Particle Swarm Optimizer. Goal is to
minimize the objective function which is the Rastrigin
benchmark function in this case
*/
import java.lang.Math;
import java.util.*;
public class ParticleSwarmOptimizer
{
// declare the variables for iterations, population size and
number of dimensions
int popSize;
int iterations;
int dimensions;
// bound variables for upper and lower bounds
double ub=5.12,lb=-5.12;
// array to hold fitness values of the solutions
double fitness[];
// array holding dimension of best solution
double[] bestSolution;
// declare dimensions of each member
double[][] positions;
double[][] positions1;
double[] pBestScore,gBest;
double[][] pBest;
```

```java
// keep best score as high. We will try and minimize this
double gBestScore=100000000;
int Vmax = 6;
double wMax = 0.9;
double wMin = 0.2;
int c1 = 2;
int c2 = 2;
/*
Constructor for initializing the population
*/
public ParticleSwarmOptimizer(int iterations,int popSize,
int dimensions)
{

    this.iterations=iterations;
    this.popSize=popSize;
    this.dimensions=dimensions;
    positions=new double[popSize][dimensions];
    positions1=new double[popSize][dimensions];

    fitness=new double[popSize];
    //initialize solutions
    // local best score
    pBestScore = new double[popSize];

    pBest = new double[popSize][dimensions];
//global best
    gBest = new double[popSize];

    for(int i=0;i<popSize;i++)
    {
        pBestScore[i]=10000000;
```

```java
    for (int j=0;j<dimensions;j++)
    {
        positions[i][j]=Math.random()*(ub-lb)+lb;
    }
    }
}

//rastrigin function used
private  double fitnessCalculator(double[] candidate)
{

    Point p= new Point(candidate);
    Rastrigin rast=new Rastrigin(10,dimensions);
    //Ackley ack=new Ackley(10,10,10,10);
    return rast.f(p);
}
/*
Optimize function for running the optimization code
*/
private void optimize()
{

    //main loop
    //loop through the population
    for(int it=0;it<iterations;it++){

        //loop over individual
        for(int i=0;i<popSize;i++)
    {
        //calculate the fitness of the individual particle
        fitness[i]=fitnessCalculator(positions[i]);

        if (pBestScore[i] > fitness[i]){
            pBestScore[i] = fitness[i];
```

```
            for(int j=0;j<dimensions;j++)
            {
            //update local best solution
        pBest[i][j] = positions[i][j];
            }

      if (gBestScore > fitness[i]){
         gBestScore = fitness[i];
            for(int j=0;j<dimensions;j++)
            {
            //update global best
        gBest[i] = positions[i][j];
            }
         }
       }

   }
      //Update the W of PSO
     double w = wMax - it * ((wMax - wMin) / iterations);
    //loop through population
    for(int i=0;i<popSize;i++)
    {
// loop through each dimension of each particle/bird
        for (int j=0;j<dimensions;j++){
            double r1 = Math.random();
            double r2 = Math.random();
// update positions as per Equation 3-1
            positions1[i][j] = (w * positions1[i][j]+
            c1 * r1 * (pBest[i][j] - positions[i][j])+
            c2 * r2 * (gBest[i] - positions[i][j]));
```

```java
            if (positions1[i][j] > Vmax)
                {
              positions1[i][j] = Vmax;
                }

            if (positions1[i][j] < -Vmax)
                {
              positions1[i][j] = -Vmax;
                }
                //update the position of the individual particle
            positions[i][j] = positions[i][j] + positions1[i][j];
             }

    }

    System.out.println("best score after iteration
    "+it+" ="+gBestScore);
}
}

 /*
Main method to take command line arguments like iterations,
population size and number of dimensions
*/
public static void main(String[] args)
{
int iter=Integer.parseInt(args[0]);
int pop=Integer.parseInt(args[1]);
int dim=Integer.parseInt(args[2]);
ParticleSwarmOptimizer pso =new ParticleSwarmOptimizer(iter,
pop,dim);
pso.optimize();
}
}
```

Executing the Completed PSO Code

To compile the Java files, please use the following commands.

```
javac Point.java
javac Rastrigin.java
javac ParticleSwarmOptimizer.java

//running the example with 50 iterations and population size of
10 and 30 dimensions
Command for running the Optimizer class is shown below
java ParticleSwarmOptimizer 50 10 30
```

The following is the output after running the code.

```
best score after iteration 0 =478.2638626565206
best score after iteration 1 =310.2955850826501
best score after iteration 2 =310.2955850826501
best score after iteration 3 =310.2955850826501
best score after iteration 4 =310.2955850826501
best score after iteration 5 =310.092438291369
best score after iteration 6 =310.092438291369
best score after iteration 7 =310.092438291369
best score after iteration 8 =310.092438291369
best score after iteration 9 =310.092438291369
best score after iteration 10 =306.3686693103556
best score after iteration 11 =306.3686693103556
best score after iteration 12 =306.3686693103556
best score after iteration 13 =286.6539375829212
best score after iteration 14 =286.6539375829212
best score after iteration 15 =233.26582419197734
best score after iteration 16 =233.26582419197734
best score after iteration 17 =233.26582419197734
best score after iteration 18 =233.26582419197734
```

```
best score after iteration 19 =233.26582419197734
best score after iteration 20 =233.26582419197734
best score after iteration 21 =206.18491064141006
best score after iteration 22 =206.18491064141006
best score after iteration 23 =206.18491064141006
best score after iteration 24 =206.18491064141006
best score after iteration 25 =203.7517447417162
best score after iteration 26 =203.7517447417162
best score after iteration 27 =203.7517447417162
best score after iteration 28 =203.7517447417162
best score after iteration 29 =203.7517447417162
best score after iteration 30 =203.7517447417162
best score after iteration 31 =203.7517447417162
best score after iteration 32 =203.7517447417162
best score after iteration 33 =203.7517447417162
best score after iteration 34 =203.7517447417162
best score after iteration 35 =203.7517447417162
best score after iteration 36 =203.7517447417162
best score after iteration 37 =190.62736084546805
best score after iteration 38 =190.62736084546805
best score after iteration 39 =190.62736084546805
best score after iteration 40 =190.62736084546805
best score after iteration 41 =190.62736084546805
best score after iteration 42 =190.62736084546805
best score after iteration 43 =190.62736084546805
best score after iteration 44 =190.62736084546805
best score after iteration 45 =190.62736084546805
best score after iteration 46 =190.62736084546805
best score after iteration 47 =190.62736084546805
best score after iteration 48 =190.62736084546805
best score after iteration 49 =190.62736084546805
```

You've just seen how the PSO algorithm works. Next, let's discuss another bird optimization-based algorithm known as the *cuckoo search*.

History: Cuckoo Search

O Cuckoo! Shall I call thee bird, or but a wandering voice?

—William Wordsworth

The cuckoo search (CS) is a metaheuristic optimization algorithm proposed by Xin-She Yang and Suash Deb in 2009. Two behaviors of cuckoo birds are used in the cuckoo search algorithm. It is based on the obligate parasitic breeding behavior of a species of cuckoo birds that lays eggs in the nests of other bird species to increase their survival and productivity. It also explains the Lévy flight movement exhibited by cuckoos and other birds, animals, and insects.

Brood Parasitism

Some cuckoo species exhibit brood parasitism behavior. Brood parasitism behavior involves laying eggs in the nest of other birds so that the other birds can incubate the cuckoos' eggs. By evolution, cuckoo birds lay eggs that are very similar in shape and color to the host birds' eggs. This allows the cuckoo bird to trick the host birds to incubate cuckoo bird eggs. The female cuckoo bird visits various nests to lay her eggs. If the host bird discovers the cuckoo egg, however, they either throw out the egg or abandon the nest to build a new one. Figure 3-3 shows a host nest with the egg of a cuckoo bird alongside the host eggs.

Figure 3-3. *Cuckoo egg*

Lévy Flight

A Lévy flight is a mathematical concept in natural processes, science, and social media. Many birds and insects exhibit Lévy flight behavior. It is a class of a stochastic process known as a *random walk*. It is characterized by movement across straight lines punctuated by sharp 90-degree turns. Along with a bit of intuition, this kind of movement allows exploration and exploitation mechanics to be used. The solution is often explored in a local neighborhood, and taking sharp turns allows exploration to happen. Figure 3-4 illustrates Lévy flight behavior.

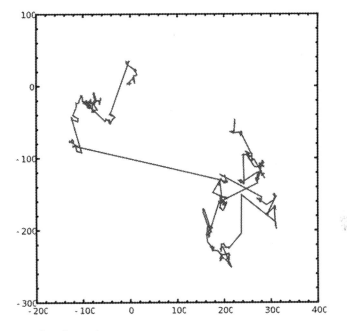

Figure 3-4. *Lévy function*

It is characterized by many random short movements and connected by infrequent large ones. Take the example of frequently visiting a favorite shop and then exploring new shops and frequenting them. The characteristic of Lévy flights is that the step lengths are chosen from a "heavy-tailed" probability distribution, which means the decreasing probabilities of longer lengths are not small enough to overpower the increasing lengths; technically, a heavy-tailed distribution has infinite variance (possible length).

Cuckoo Search Optimization (CSO) Algorithm

In a simplistic formulation, the cuckoo search algorithm has the following assumptions

- Each host nest has one egg, and each egg represents a solution in the search space.

- There is a fixed number of host nests, which is the population of the solutions.

- The cuckoo bird lays an egg, which is the new solution. The cuckoo randomly replaces an egg in a different nest with its egg. This is tantamount to replacing an old solution with a new one.

- The best nests with high-quality eggs (solutions) carry over to the next generation.

- The probability of discovering a cuckoo egg is represented by p. A fraction of the total nests are thrown away in each iteration. This means a fraction of the bad solutions are thrown away.

Let's start with a population of N solutions.

$(X_1, X_2, \ldots X_N)$ represent the population of solutions within a search space. Each solution has D dimensions. Each iteration creates a new solution by updating the existing solution. The Lévy function performs the update (see Equation 3-3).

$$X(t+1)=X(t)+c.L(u)$$

Equation 3-3. *Update to the solution*

The solution at time $t+1$ is updated by updating the solution at time t by applying the Lévy flight to it. L(u) is the Lévy distribution that models the transition probability, thus making the next position depend on the present position and the transition probability (see Equation 3-4).

$$L(u)= t^{-u} \text{ where } 1 <= u <= 3$$

Equation 3-4. *Lévy function*

Here you can see the Lévy flight operator allows searching by both exploitation and exploration. Making the step size large allows the solution to explore. Keeping the step size small allows more exploitation of the space.

In a larger step size, the search doesn't get stuck in a local optimal and comes out of it quickly. The probability parameter controls how much is explored and how much is exploited. So, p=.2 means 20% exploiting and 80% exploring.

CSO Flowchart

Figure 3-5 depicts the cuckoo search algorithm. It starts by initializing the population and other parameters, such as the number of iterations. During each iteration, the fitness of each nest (called a *solution*) is calculated. The solution with the best fit at the end of all iterations is chosen.

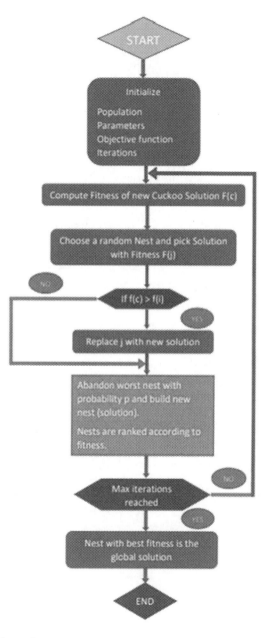

Figure 3-5. *Flowchart*

CSO Pseudocode

The following pseudocode describes the cuckoo search algorithm, as outlined in Figure 3-5.

```
Initialize
    Create N nests
    Create 1 solution in each nest. Each solution has D
    dimensions . Initialize the dimension randomly
    Define number of iterations we should run the process
Iterate
In each iteration
    Generate a new cuckoo solution using Levy flight (Cn)
    Calculate fitness (Fc)
    Choose a random nest j and pick a solution with Fitness Fj
    If (Fc>Fj)
        Replace j by new solution
    End if
    Abandon worst nest with probability p and build new
    nest (solution)
    Nests are ranked according to fitness
    Nest with best fitness is ranked the current best
Iterate till the max iterations configured
Nest with best fitness is the global best solution
```

CSO Prerequisites and Code

Again, make sure that Java 8 (JDK8 or higher) is installed on your computer. An IDE like Eclipse is recommended but not necessary because you can use the command-line interface to run the code without an IDE.

The code for the CSO algorithm contains the following classes.

- Point is the utility class with three members (see Listing 3-4).

  - A double

  - An array of integers

  - An integer

- Rastrigin is the utility class for the optimization evaluation function (see Listing 3-5). The Rastrigin benchmark function is shown in Equation 3-4.

$$f(\mathbf{x}) = An + \sum_{i=1}^{n} \left[x_i^2 - A\cos(2\pi x_i) \right]$$

$$\text{where: } A = 10$$

Equation 3-4. *Rastrigin benchmark function*

- The CuckooSearchDataHolder class serves as a data holder (see Listing 3-6). It holds the best solution, array of nests, and the fitness values of each nest.

- The CuckooSearchOptimizer class is the main Java class (see Listing 3-7). It optimizes by minimizing the objective function represented by the Rastrigin benchmark function.

As in the previous section, I've added comments within the code.

Listing 3-4. The Point Class

```
public class Point {
    public double p[];
    public int ip[];
    public int dim;

    public Point(double p[]) {
        this.dim = p.length;
        this.p = p.clone();
    }

    public Point(int p[]) {
        this.dim = p.length;
        this.ip = p.clone();
    }

    public Point(int dim) {
        this.dim = dim;
        p = new double[dim];
    }
    /*
    this method returns the square root of the sum of the
    square of the members in the array of doubles
    */
    public double norm(){
        double sum = 0;
        for (int i = 0; i < dim ; i ++) {
            sum += Math.pow(this.p[i], 2);
        }
        return Math.sqrt(sum);
    }
```

```
/*
This method returns the square root of the distance between
2 points. Its calculated by taking sum of the square of the
distance between each element of the double array and then
doing a square root of it.
*/
public double dist(Point b){
    double sum = 0;
    for (int i = 0; i < dim ; i ++) {
        sum += Math.pow(this.p[i]-b.p[i], 2);
    }
    return Math.sqrt(sum);
}
/*
This method adds the two Points by taking sum of the
individual elements of the double array of each Point
*/

public static Point add(Point a, Point b) throws Exception
{
    if (a.dim != b.dim){
        throw new IllegalArgumentException("Adding points
        from different dimensions");
    }
    int dim  = a.dim;
    double cp[] = new double[dim];
    for (int i = 0; i < dim; i++){
        cp[i] = a.p[i] + b.p[i];
    }
    return new Point(cp);
}
```

```
/*
This method adds the two Points by taking sum of the
individual elements of the double array of each Point and
then takes an average of each added elements and finally
returns a Point with the averages points in the new array
*/

public static Point mid(Point a, Point b) throws Exception{
    if (a.dim != b.dim){
        throw new IllegalArgumentException
        ("Incompatible points");
    }
    int dim  = a.dim;
    double cor[] = new double[dim];
    for (int i = 0; i < dim; i++){
        cor[i] = (a.p[i] + b.p[i]) / 2.0;
    }
    return new Point (cor);
}
/*
This method multiplies each element of the array of double
with the constant a. a is the coefficient we use in the
optimization algorithm.
*/
public Point mull(double a) {
    double p[] = new double[this.dim];
    Point m = new Point(p);
    for (int i = 0; i < this.dim; i++){
        m.p[i] = this.p[i]*a;
    }
    return m;
}
```

```java
/*
This method returns a string representation of the double
array
*/

@Override
public String toString() {
    if (p != null) {
        String s = "[";
        for (int i = 0; i < this.dim; i++){
            s += (float)p[i];
            if (i == this.dim - 1) {
                s += "]";
            } else {
                s += ",";
            }
        }
        return s;
    } else {
        String s = "[";
        for (int i = 0; i < this.dim; i++){
            s += (int)ip[i];
            if (i == this.dim - 1) {
                s += "]";
            } else {
                s += ",";
            }
        }
        return s;
    }
}
}
```

Listing 3-5. The Rastrigin Class

```
/*
This class is used as the benchmark function and will be
used throughout all algorithms.

*/
public class Rastrigin {

    private double A;
    private double n;

    public Rastrigin(double A, double n) {
        this.A = A;
        this.n = n;
    }

    /*
    This method is the main method for the Rastrigin benchmark
    function. It takes as input a Point object (explained
    above) and performs the calculations for the benchmark.
     */

    public double f(Point x) {
        double sum = 0;
        //o = numpy.sum(x ** 2 - 10 * numpy.cos
        (2 * math.pi * x)) + 10 * dim
        for (int i = 0; i < x.dim; i++) {

            sum += Math.pow(x.p[i], 2) - A*Math.cos
            (2*Math.PI*x.p[i]);
```

```
    }
    return A*n + sum;
  }
}
```

Listing 3-6. The CuckooSearchDataHolder Class

```
/*
A data holder class for holding the best solution, array of
nests and the fitness values of each nest.
*/
public class CuckooSearchDataHolder
{
 double fNew;
double[] best;
double[][]nest;
 double[]fitness;
 public CuckooSearchDataHolder(double fNew,double[]
 best,double[][]nest,double[]fitness)
 {
    this.fNew=fNew;
    this.best=best;
    this.nest=nest;
    this.fitness=fitness;
 }
}
```

Listing 3-7. The CuckooSearch Class

```
/*
This class optimizes by minimizing the objective function
represented by the Rastrigin benchmark function
*/

import java.lang.Math;
import java.util.*;
public class CuckooSearch
{
// declare the iterations, population size and the dimensions
variables
int popSize;
int iterations;

int dimensions;
// declare and initialize lower and upper bounds
double ub=5.12,lb=-5.12;
double fitness[];
double[] bestSolution;
//coefficients and constants for the algo
double beta = 1.5;
//discovery rate of alien/egg solution
double pa = 0.25;
double minValueOfSolution;
double leaderDistance;
double[][] positions;
List solutionCurve;

public CuckooSearch(int iterations,int popSize, int dimensions)
{
    solutionCurve=new ArrayList();
    this.iterations=iterations;
```

```java
    this.popSize=popSize;
    this.dimensions=dimensions;
    positions=new double[popSize][dimensions];

    fitness=new double[popSize];
    //initialize solutions
    for(int i=0;i<popSize;i++)
    {
    for (int j=0;j<dimensions;j++)
    {
        //System.out.println("i="+i+"j="+j);
        positions[i][j]=Math.random()*(ub-lb)+lb;
    }
    }
    for(int i=0;i<popSize;i++)
    {
        //passing high fitness to start with
        fitness[i]=100000;
        System.out.println("fitness for "+i +" solution="+
        fitness[i]);
    }

}
/*
Sigma function for standard variance
*/
private double doSigma(){
    double term1 = this.logGamma(beta+1)*Math.sin
    ((Math.PI*beta)/2);
    double term2 = this.logGamma((beta+1)/2)*beta*Math.
    pow(2,(beta-1)/2);
    return Math.pow((term1/term2),(1/beta));
    }
```

```
private Double logGamma(double x){
   double tmp = (x - 0.5) * Math.log(x + 4.5) - (x + 4.5);
   double ser = 1.0 + 76.18009173    / (x + 0)    -
   86.50532033    / (x + 1)
            + 24.01409822     / (x + 2)    -
            1.231739516    / (x + 3)
            +  0.00120858003 / (x + 4)    -
            0.00000536382 / (x + 5);
   return Math.exp(tmp + Math.log(ser * Math.sqrt
   (2 * Math.PI)));
}
/*
Replace few nests from the initial population of nests
*/
private double[][] emptyNests(double[][] nest, double pa){

   double[][] tmpPositions=nest.clone();

   int k;
   if(Math.random()>pa)
   {
       k=1;
   }
   else
       k=0;

   for(int i=0;i<popSize;i++)
   {
       double tmp1[]=nest[i].clone();
       double tmp2[]=nest[i].clone();
       Collections.shuffle(Arrays.asList(tmp1));
       Collections.shuffle(Arrays.asList(tmp2));
```

```java
        for(int j=0;j<dimensions;j++)
    {

    double stepsize =Math.random()*(tmp1[j]-tmp2[j])*k;
    tmpPositions[i][j]=nest[i][j]+stepsize;
    }
    }

    return tmpPositions;

}
/*
Return a nest by performing a levy flight.
*/
private double[][] getCuckooNest(double[][] nest, double[] best){

    // perform Levy flights

    double[][] tmpPositions=nest.clone();

    double beta = 3 / 2;
    double sigma = doSigma();

    double[] s = new double[dimensions];
    System.out.println("lent="+nest.length);

    for (int j =0;j<nest.length;j++)
    {
        s=nest[j].clone();
        Random rnd=new Random();

        double u= rnd.nextGaussian()*sigma ;
        double v = rnd.nextGaussian();
        double step = u / Math.abs(v) * (1 / beta);
```

```
    for (int k=0;k<dimensions;k++)
      {
          double x=s[k]- best[k];
          double  stepsize = 0.01 * (step * x);

          double y= stepsize * rnd.nextGaussian();
          s[k]=s[k]+y;
      tmpPositions[j][k] = clipVal(s[k],lb,ub);
      }
    }
    return tmpPositions;

}
/*
Get the best fit nest
*/
private CuckooSearchDataHolder getBestNest(double[][]nest,
double[][]newnest, double[]fitness){
    // Evaluating all new solutions
    double[][] tmpPositions=nest.clone();
    for(int j=0;j<popSize;j++)
    {

     double fNew=fitnessCalculator(newnest[j]);

       if (fNew <= fitness[j])
         {
         fitness[j] = fNew;
         tmpPositions[j] = newnest[j];

         }
    }
    // Find the current best
```

```
    int bestIndex= indexOfSmallest(fitness);
    bestSolution=tmpPositions[bestIndex];
    minValueOfSolution=smallestInArray(fitness);

    CuckooSearchDataHolder    csdh=new CuckooSearchData
    Holder(minValueOfSolution,bestSolution,tmpPositions,
    fitness);
return csdh;
    }

private double clipVal(double val,double lower,double upper)
{
    double result;
      if (val < lower){
        result = lower;

        }
      else if (val > upper){
        result = upper;

        }
        else
        {
            result=val;

        }
    return result;
}

//rastrigin function used
private  double fitnessCalculator(double[] candidate)
{

    Point p= new Point(candidate);
    Rastrigin rast=new Rastrigin(10,dimensions);
```

```java
    //Ackley ack=new Ackley(10,10,10,10);
    return rast.f(p);
}
/*
Helper method which finds the smallest member in an array of
doubles
*/

private static double smallestInArray(double[] array){

    // add this
    if (array.length == 0)
      return -1;

    int index = 0;
    double min = array[index];

    for (int i = 1; i < array.length; i++){
      if (array[i] <= min){
      min = array[i];
      //index = i;
      }
    }
    return min;
}
/*
Helper method which finds the index of the smallest member in
an array of doubles
*/

private static int indexOfSmallest(double[] array){

    // add this
    if (array.length == 0)
      return -1;
```

```
    int index = 0;
    double min = array[index];

    for (int i = 1; i < array.length; i++){
      if (array[i] <= min){
      min = array[i];
      index = i;
      }
    }
    return index;
}
/*
Main method for running the Cuckoo Search algorithm
*/

private void optimize()
{
    //main loop
    //bestSolution is initialized

    CuckooSearchDataHolder csdh=getBestNest(positions,
    positions.clone(),fitness);

    for(int i=0;i<iterations;i++){
        //loop over individual
        // get a nest by performing a Levy flight
    CuckooSearchDataHolder csdh1;
        double[][] newNest=getCuckooNest(csdh.nest,csdh.best);
        // get best nest by evaluating the fitness function
        csdh1=getBestNest(positions,newNest,csdh.fitness);
        // create some new nests and discard some old nests
         newNest = emptyNests(newNest, pa);
```

```
    // get best nest by evaluating the fitness function

    csdh1=getBestNest(positions,newNest,csdh1.fitness);

    //fnew, best, nest, fitness = get_best_nest(nest,
      new_nest, fitness, n, dim, objf)

        if (csdh1.fNew < csdh.fNew)
        {
        csdh.fNew = csdh1.fNew;
            csdh.best = csdh1.best;

        }

        for(int j=0;j<popSize;j++)
        {

        System.out.println("iter="+i+" best fitness is ="+csdh.
        fNew);
        solutionCurve.add(minValueOfSolution);
    }

}
for (int i=0;i< solutionCurve.size();i++)
        {
            System.out.println("\n"+solutionCurve.get(i));
        }
}
/*
Main method to pass inputs and launch the algorithm
*/
//takes input as number of iterations, population size and
dimensions
```

```
public static void main(String[] args)
{

int iter=Integer.parseInt(args[0]);
int pop=Integer.parseInt(args[1]);
int dim=Integer.parseInt(args[2]);
CuckooSearch cuckoo =new CuckooSearch(iter,pop,dim);
cuckoo.optimize();
}
}
```

Executing the Code

To compile the Java files, please use the following commands.

```
javac Point.java
javac Rastrigin.java
javac CuckooSearchDataHolder.java
javac CuckooSearch.java
```

```
//running the example with 50 iterations and population size of
10 and 30 dimensions
java CuckooSearch 50 10 30
```

Output

The following is the output after running the code.

```
iter=0 best fitness is =465.6496390625076
iter=1 best fitness is =465.6496390625076
iter=2 best fitness is =465.6496390625076
iter=3 best fitness is =465.6496390625076
```

```
iter=4 best fitness is =465.6496390625076
iter=5 best fitness is =465.6496390625076
iter=6 best fitness is =465.6496390625076
```

iter=7 best fitness is =465.6496390625076

```
iter=8 best fitness is =465.6496390625076
iter=9 best fitness is =465.6496390625076
iter=10 best fitness is =465.6496390625076
iter=11 best fitness is =465.6496390625076
iter=12 best fitness is =465.6496390625076
iter=13 best fitness is =465.6496390625076
iter=14 best fitness is =465.6496390625076
iter=15 best fitness is =465.6496390625076
iter=16 best fitness is =465.6496390625076
iter=17 best fitness is =465.6496390625076
iter=18 best fitness is =465.6496390625076
iter=19 best fitness is =465.6496390625076
iter=20 best fitness is =465.6496390625076
iter=21 best fitness is =465.6496390625076
iter=22 best fitness is =465.6496390625076
iter=23 best fitness is =465.6496390625076
iter=24 best fitness is =465.6496390625076
iter=25 best fitness is =465.6496390625076
iter=26 best fitness is =465.6496390625076
iter=27 best fitness is =465.6496390625076
iter=28 best fitness is =465.6496390625076
iter=29 best fitness is =465.6496390625076
iter=30 best fitness is =465.6496390625076
iter=31 best fitness is =465.6496390625076
iter=32 best fitness is =465.6496390625076
iter=33 best fitness is =465.6496390625076
iter=34 best fitness is =465.6496390625076
```

```
iter=35 best fitness is =465.6496390625076
iter=36 best fitness is =465.6496390625076
iter=37 best fitness is =464.14178857501577
iter=38 best fitness is =464.14178857501577
iter=39 best fitness is =464.14178857501577
iter=40 best fitness is =464.14178857501577
iter=41 best fitness is =464.14178857501577
iter=42 best fitness is =464.14178857501577
iter=43 best fitness is =464.14178857501577
iter=44 best fitness is =464.14178857501577
iter=45 best fitness is =458.7217674665756
iter=46 best fitness is =443.12284759917725
iter=47 best fitness is =443.12284759917725
iter=48 best fitness is =443.12284759917725
iter=49 best fitness is =443.12284759917725
```

Summary

This chapter introduced optimization problem solutions specific to a class of birds, particularly particle swarm optimization and cuckoo search optimization. It covered the basic flow of an optimization problem and solution and presented flowcharts, pseudocodes, and code written in Java. The Rastrigin benchmark function was used as the objective function in the algorithms.

CHAPTER 4

Insects: Firefly Optimization

The fireflies o'er the meadow in pulses come and go.

— James Russell Lowell

This chapter introduces you to optimization problem-solving with fireflies. You learn how fireflies have developed specific techniques for flashing based on the intensity of the light around them. The firefly algorithm is a metaheuristic algorithm in which the search space is based on exploration and exploitation.

History

Fireflies are insects that belong to the Lampyridae family in the beetle order Coleoptera. They are sometimes known colloquially as *lightning bugs*. Most species are nocturnal and spend the day hidden under leaves or in crevices. They are small, with a length of 4 to 9 millimeters and an average weight of 3 to 6 milligrams. Lightning bugs live in damp places— beneath trees, in rotting wood, under stones, beneath bark, and between the joints of trees and shrubs. Most species are not aggressive or territorial, having adapted to living near each other.

© Shashank Jain 2022
S. Jain, *Nature-Inspired Optimization Algorithms with Java*,
https://doi.org/10.1007/978-1-4842-7401-9_4

Fireflies exhibit flashing behaviors during twilight and at night. They rhythmically flash their abdomens for a duration of about a second in a five- to ten-second pattern. Flashing is an important component in the mating process of fireflies; it allows males to signal females.

There is a long observation history of lightning bugs in the wild. Many ancient cultures have referred to lightning bugs as the "spirit of the night."

The two behaviors inspire firefly optimization.

- Flashing

- Lévy flight

A Lévy flight is a stochastic random walk discussed in the Chapter 3.

Algorithm

There are three basic assumptions on which the firefly algorithm works.

- All fireflies are unisex, which means any firefly can be attracted to any other firefly depending on the flash brightness of the corresponding firefly.

- The brightness of an individual firefly is determined by its fitness function.

- The attractiveness of a firefly depends on the intensity of the light it emits. A firefly always moves toward a more attractive firefly. If there is no other attractive (bright) firefly, then it just moves randomly. Attractiveness decreases as the distance between fireflies increases.

Since the intensity of light is inversely proportional to the square of the distance from the source, Equation 4-1 defines attractiveness.

$$B(r)=B(0)e^{-gr2}$$

Equation 4-1. *Defining attractiveness*

The attractiveness at distance r, $(B(r))$ is determined by the attractiveness at $B(0)$). If a firefly located at X_j is more attractive than a firefly at X_i, the firefly at X_i moves toward X_j.

The firefly's position update at X_i is described by Equation 4-2.

$$X_i^{t+1} = X_i^t + \beta_0 e^{-\gamma r_{ij}^2} \left(X_j^t - X_i^t \right) + \alpha_t \in_i^t$$

Equation 4-2 *Firefly position updating*

The right side of the equation has three parts for a firefly at location X.

- The position of the firefly at iteration t.

- The attractiveness of the firefly at location j.

- Alpha is a random term, and epsilon is a random number drawn from a Gaussian, uniform, or Lévy distribution.

Flowchart

This section describes the firefly optimization algorithm. At a high level, it involves initializing parameters, such as the firefly population or the number of iterations (see Figure 4-1). The fireflies' positions are updated during each iteration based on the intensity of emitted light from other fireflies, and their fitness is calculated. At the end of the final iteration, the best fit solution is chosen.

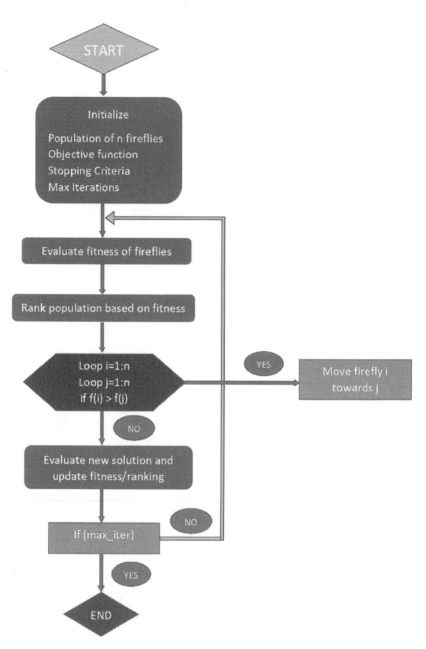

Figure 4-1. *Flowchart for the firefly optimization algorithm*

Pseudocode

The following pseudocode describes the firefly optimization algorithm, as outlined in Figure 4-1.

```
Initialize
    Initialize the population of fireflies
    Randomly assign a location to each firefly
    Define the fitness function (its same as the intensity of
    light emitted)
Iterate
    Loop over the population of fireflies (for i=1 to N)
        Start another loop of fireflies (for j=1 to N)
        Calculate fitness f(i) and f(j)
        If (f(i)>f(j))
        Move firefly j towards firefly i
        endif
        Update intensity of fireflies as they take new positions
        End inner for loop
    End outer for loop
    Rank the fireflies as per their fitness values
    Keep iterating till max value of iterations is reached
Firefly with max fitness is the global optima.
```

Prerequisites and Code

Make sure that Java 8 (JDK8 or higher) is installed on your computer. An IDE like Eclipse is recommended but not necessary because you can use the command-line interface to run the code without an IDE.

The code for the firefly algorithm consists of the following classes.

- The Point utility class, with three members (see Listing 4-1)

  - A double array

  - An array of integers

  - An integer

- The Rastrigin utility class for the optimization evaluation function (see Listing 4-2)

- The ArrayUtils class for utility functions (see Listing 4-3)

- The FireflyOptimizer optimization class, the main Java class for the functionality of the algorithm (see Listing 4-4)

The Rastrigin benchmark function for the firefly algorithm is shown in Equation 4-3.

$$f(\mathbf{x}) = An + \sum_{i=1}^{n} \left[x_i^2 - A\cos(2\pi x_i) \right]$$

$$\text{where: } A = 10$$

Equation 4-3. *Rastrigin benchmark function*

Listing 4-1. The Point Class

```java
public class Point {
    public double p[];
    public int ip[];
    public int dim;

    public Point(double p[]) {
        this.dim = p.length;
        this.p = p.clone();
    }

    public Point(int p[]) {
        this.dim = p.length;
        this.ip = p.clone();
    }

    public Point(int dim) {
        this.dim = dim;
        p = new double[dim];
    }
    /*
    this method returns the square root of the sum of the
    square of the members in the array of doubles
    */
    public double norm(){
        double sum = 0;
        for (int i = 0; i < dim ; i ++) {
            sum += Math.pow(this.p[i], 2);
        }
        return Math.sqrt(sum);
    }
```

```
/*
This method returns the square root of the distance
between 2 points. It's calculated by taking sum of the
square of the distance between each element of the double
array and then doing a square root of it.
*/
public double dist(Point b){
    double sum = 0;
    for (int i = 0; i < dim ; i ++) {
        sum += Math.pow(this.p[i]-b.p[i], 2);
    }
    return Math.sqrt(sum);
}
/*
This method adds the two Points by taking sum of the
individual elements of the double array of each Point
*/

public static Point add(Point a, Point b) throws Exception {
    if (a.dim != b.dim){
        throw new IllegalArgumentException("Adding points
        from different dimensions");
    }
    int dim  = a.dim;
    double cp[] = new double[dim];
    for (int i = 0; i < dim; i++){
        cp[i] = a.p[i] + b.p[i];
    }
    return new Point(cp);
}
```

```
/*
This method adds the two Points by taking sum of the
individual elements of the double array of each Point and
then takes an average of each added elements and finally
returns a Point with the averages points in the new array
*/

public static Point mid(Point a, Point b) throws Exception{
    if (a.dim != b.dim){
        throw new IllegalArgumentException
        ("Incompatible points");
    }
    int dim  = a.dim;
    double cor[] = new double[dim];
    for (int i = 0; i < dim; i++){
        cor[i] = (a.p[i] + b.p[i]) / 2.0;
    }
    return new Point (cor);
}
/*
This method multiplies each element of the array of double
with the constant a. a is the coefficient we use in the
optimization algorithm.
*/
public Point mull(double a) {
    double p[] = new double[this.dim];
    Point m = new Point(p);
    for (int i = 0; i < this.dim; i++){
        m.p[i] = this.p[i]*a;
    }
    return m;
}
```

```
/*
This method returns a string representation of the double
array
*/

@Override
public String toString() {
    if (p != null) {
        String s = "[";
        for (int i = 0; i < this.dim; i++){
            s += (float)p[i];
            if (i == this.dim - 1) {
                s += "]";
            } else {
                s += ",";
            }
        }
        return s;
    } else {
        String s = "[";
        for (int i = 0; i < this.dim; i++){
            s += (int)ip[i];
            if (i == this.dim - 1) {
                s += "]";
            } else {
                s += ",";
            }
        }
        return s;
    }
}
}// end of Point class
```

Listing 4-2. The Rastrigin Benchmark Function Class

```
/*
This class is used as the benchmark function and will be
used throughout all algorithms.

*/
public class Rastrigin {

    private double A;
    private double n;

    public Rastrigin(double A, double n) {
        this.A = A;
        this.n = n;
    }

    /*
    This method is the main method for the Rastrigin benchmark
    function. It takes as input a Point object (explained
    above) and performs the calculations for the benchmark.
     */

    public double f(Point x) {
        double sum = 0;
        //o = numpy.sum(x ** 2 - 10 * numpy.cos
        (2 * math.pi * x)) + 10 * dim
        for (int i = 0; i < x.dim; i++) {

            sum += Math.pow(x.p[i], 2) - A*Math.cos(
            2*Math.PI*x.p[i]);

        }
        return A*n + sum;
    }
}//end of Rastrigin class
```

Listing 4-3. The ArrayUtils Utility Class

```
import java.util.Arrays;
import java.util.Comparator;
import java.util.Random;

public final class ArrayUtils {
    public static int[] argsort(final double[] a) {
        return argsort(a, true);
    }
/*
Arg sort method . This returns indices which would sort the array
*/
    public static int[] argsort(final double[] a, final boolean
    ascending) {
        Integer[] indexes = new Integer[a.length];
        for (int i = 0; i < indexes.length; i++) {
            indexes[i] = i;
        }
        Arrays.sort(indexes, new Comparator<Integer>() {
            @Override
            public int compare(final Integer i1, final
            Integer i2) {
                return (ascending ? 1 : -1) * Double.
                compare(a[i1], a[i2]);
            }
        });
        return asArray(indexes);
    }

    public static <T extends Number> int[] asArray
    (final T... a) {
        int[] b = new int[a.length];
```

```
    for (int i = 0; i < b.length; i++) {
        b[i] = a[i].intValue();
    }
    return b;
}

public static double[] castOf(final double[] x) {
    double[] y = new double[x.length];
    for (int i = 0; i < y.length; i++) {
        y[i] = x[i];
    }
    return y;
}

public static int[] castOf(final long[] original) {
    return castOf(original, original.length);
}

public static int[] castOf(final long[] original, final int
newLength) {
    int[] cast = new int[newLength];
    int length = Math.min(cast.length, original.length);
    for (int i = 0; i < length; i++) {
        long o = original[i];
        if (o < Integer.MIN_VALUE || o > Integer.MAX_VALUE) {
            throw new IllegalArgumentException();
        }
        cast[i] = (int) o;
    }
    return cast;
}
```

```
/*
Copies the array  upto the length specified.
*/
    public static double[][] copyOf(final double[][] x, final
    int newLength) {
        double[][] y = new double[newLength][];
        for (int i = 0; i < y.length; i++) {
            if (x[i] != null) {
                y[i] = Arrays.copyOf(x[i], x[i].length);
            }
        }
        return y;
    }

    /**
    * Assigns a random value to each element of the specified
      array of doubles.
    */
    public static void fillRandom(final double[] x, final
    Random rng) {
        for (int i = 0; i < x.length; i++) {
            x[i] = rng.nextDouble();
        }
    }

    private ArrayUtils() {
    }
}//end of ArrayUtils class
```

The FireflyOptimizer class in Listing 4-4 is the main class for the optimizer's functionality. It uses other classes, like Point, Rastrigin, and ArrayUtils.

Listing 4-4. The FireflyOptimizer Class

```java
import java.lang.Math;
import java.util.*;
public class FireFlyOptimizer
{
// declare the number of iterations, population size and
dimensions
int popSize;
int iterations;
int dimensions;
// declare the bounds for upper and lower values
double ub=5.12,lb=-5.12;
double fitness[];
double[] bestSolution;
// declare variables for coefficients and constants
double alpha = 0.5 ; // Randomness 0--1 (highly random)
double betamin = 0.20 ; // minimum value of beta
double gamma = 1  ;// Absorption coefficient
double minValueOfSolution;
double[][] positions;
double[][] positions1;
int[] sortedIndex;

public FireFlyOptimizer(int iterations,int popSize, int
dimensions)
{
    // initialize the population
    this.iterations=iterations;
    this.popSize=popSize;
    this.dimensions=dimensions;
    positions=new double[popSize][dimensions];
```

```
    positions1=new double[popSize][dimensions];
    fitness=new double[popSize];
    //initialize solutions

    for(int i=0;i<popSize;i++)
    {
    for (int j=0;j<dimensions;j++)
    {

        positions[i][j]=Math.random()*(ub-lb)+lb;

        positions[i][j]=clipVal(positions[i][j],lb,ub);
    }
    }
}
/*
Method to Clip the values between lower and upper bounds
*/
private double clipVal(double val,double lower,double upper)
{
    double result;
      if (val < lower){
        result = lower;

        }
      else if (val > upper){
        result = upper;

        }
        else
        {
            result=val;

        }
```

```java
        return result;
}
//rastrigin function used
private  double fitnessCalculator(double[] candidate)
{

    Point p= new Point(candidate);
    Rastrigin rast=new Rastrigin(10,dimensions);
    //Ackley ack=new Ackley(10,10,10,10);
    return rast.f(p);
}
/*
Helper method which finds the index of the smallest member in
an array of doubles
*/

private static int indexOfSmallest(double[] array){
    // add this
    if (array.length == 0)
        return -1;

    int index = 0;
    double min = array[index];

    for (int i = 1; i < array.length; i++){
        if (array[i] <= min){
        min = array[i];
        index = i;
        }
    }
    return index;
}
```

```
/*
Method to update firefly positions based on fitness
*/
private void updateFireFlies(int iterations)
{
        double alpha1=getAlpha(alpha,iterations);
      double[] scale = new double[dimensions];

      double[] fireflies=new double[popSize];
      //loop through all fireflies
      for(int i=0;i<popSize;i++)
      {
      // inner loop for fireflies
          for(int j=0;j<popSize;j++)
      {
          double sum=0;
          double r=0;
          for(int k=0;k<dimensions;k++)
          {
              double diff=positions[i][k]-positions[j][k];
              sum=sum+diff;
              r=Math.pow(sum,2);

          }
      // if fitness of i(th) firefly  greater then j(th) firefly
          if(fitness[i]>fitness[j])
          {
              double beta0 = 1;
          double beta = (beta0 - betamin) * Math.exp(-gamma
          * Math.pow(r , 2)) + betamin;
```

```
                double tmpf[]=new double[dimensions];

                    for(int k=0;k<dimensions;k++)
            {

                    tmpf[k] = alpha1 * (Math.
                    random()*dimensions - 0.5) * scale[k];
//keep updating the position of the firefly
positions[i][k] = positions[i][k]* (1 - beta) + positions1[j]
[k] * beta + tmpf[k];

                }
                }

        }
        }

}
/*
Method for reducing alpha value
*/
private double  getAlpha(double alpha, int gen){

    double  delta = 1 - Math.pow((Math.pow(10,-4) / 0.9) ,
    (1 / gen));
    alpha = (1 - delta) * alpha;
    return alpha;
}

/*
Method for optimizing
*/
```

```java
private void optimize()
{
    //main loop for starting the iterations
    for(int it=0;it<iterations;it++){
        //loop over individual  firefly

        for(int i=0;i<popSize;i++)
    {
        // calculate the fitness of the firefly based on position
        fitness[i]=fitnessCalculator(positions[i]);

    }
    int bestIndex= indexOfSmallest(fitness);

    bestSolution=positions[bestIndex];

    minValueOfSolution=fitness[bestIndex];
    System.out.println("best solution at iteration
    "+it+"="+minValueOfSolution);
    sortedIndex=ArrayUtils.argsort(fitness,true);

    for(int x=0;x<sortedIndex.length;x++)
    {
        for(int y=0;y<dimensions;y++)
        {
            int p=sortedIndex[x];
            positions1[p][y]=positions[p][y];
        }

    }
        // update the firefly positions based on existing positions
        updateFireFlies(iterations);

}

}
```

```
/*
Main method to pass inputs and launch the algorithm
*/

public static void main(String[] args)
{
//takes input as number of iterations, population size and
dimensions

int iter=Integer.parseInt(args[0]);
int pop=Integer.parseInt(args[1]);
int dim=Integer.parseInt(args[2]);
FireFlyOptimizer firefly =new FireFlyOptimizer(iter,pop,dim);
firefly.optimize();
}
}
```

Executing the Code

Let's compile the source code and execute it. The following are the commands for compiling the Java files.

```
javac Point.java
javac Rastrigin.java
javac ArrayUtils.java
javac FireFlyOptimizer.java
```

```
//running the example with 50 iterations and population size of
10 and 30 dimensions
The following command is used for running the code.
java FireFlyOptimizer 50 10 30
```

Output

After executing the code, you see the following results.

```
best solution at iteration 0=531.4740994175238
best solution at iteration 1=305.28766121650875
best solution at iteration 2=286.9754494150518
best solution at iteration 3=262.68691724344035
best solution at iteration 4=262.5778766205223
best solution at iteration 5=262.5778766205223
best solution at iteration 6=262.53064502982664
best solution at iteration 7=262.53064502982664
best solution at iteration 8=262.53064502982664
best solution at iteration 9=262.53064502982664
best solution at iteration 10=262.53064502982664
best solution at iteration 11=262.53064502982664
best solution at iteration 12=262.53064502982664
best solution at iteration 13=262.53064502982664
best solution at iteration 14=262.53064502982664
best solution at iteration 15=262.53064502982664
best solution at iteration 16=262.53064502982664
best solution at iteration 17=262.53064502982664
best solution at iteration 18=262.53064502982664
best solution at iteration 19=262.53064502982664
best solution at iteration 20=262.53064502982664
best solution at iteration 21=262.53064502982664
best solution at iteration 22=262.53064502982664
best solution at iteration 23=262.53064502982664
best solution at iteration 24=262.53064502982664
best solution at iteration 25=262.53064502982664
best solution at iteration 26=262.53064502982664
best solution at iteration 27=262.53064502982664
```

```
best solution at iteration 28=262.53064502982664
best solution at iteration 29=262.53064502982664
best solution at iteration 30=262.53064502982664
best solution at iteration 31=262.53064502982664
best solution at iteration 32=262.53064502982664
best solution at iteration 33=262.53064502982664
best solution at iteration 34=262.53064502982664
best solution at iteration 35=262.53064502982664
best solution at iteration 36=262.53064502982664
best solution at iteration 37=262.53064502982664
best solution at iteration 38=262.53064502982664
best solution at iteration 39=262.53064502982664
best solution at iteration 40=262.53064502982664
best solution at iteration 41=262.53064502982664
best solution at iteration 42=262.53064502982664
best solution at iteration 43=262.53064502982664
best solution at iteration 44=262.53064502982664
best solution at iteration 45=262.53064502982664
best solution at iteration 46=262.53064502982664
best solution at iteration 47=262.53064502982664
best solution at iteration 48=262.53064502982664
best solution at iteration 49=262.53064502982664
```

Summary

This chapter introduced the optimization problem solutions specific to fireflies and their flashing behavior. It covered the basic flow of an optimization problem and solution and presented a corresponding flowchart, pseudocode, and code written in Java. The Rastrigin benchmark function was used as the objective function in the algorithms.

CHAPTER 5

Sea Creatures: Salp Swarm Optimization

This chapter introduces you to the salp swarm optimization method, which is another metaheuristic technique. The optimization belongs to a class of animals that live under the sea.

History

Salps belong to the Salpidae family. They have a transparent barrel-shaped body, and their tissues are highly similar to jellyfishes. They move like jellyfish in that water is pumped through the body as propulsion to move forward.

Biological research about these creatures is in its early stages, mainly because their living environments are extremely difficult to access, and it is difficult to keep them in laboratory environments.

One of the most interesting behaviors of salps involves their swarming. In deep oceans, salps often form a swarm called a *salp chain*. The main reason for this behavior is not very clear yet, but some researchers believe it is done to achieve better locomotion using rapid coordinated changes and foraging.

Salp chains are primarily divided into two parts.

- The first salp in the chain is the *leader*.

- All the other salps in the chain are *followers*.

© Shashank Jain 2022
S. Jain, *Nature-Inspired Optimization Algorithms with Java*,
https://doi.org/10.1007/978-1-4842-7401-9_5

Salp Swarm Algorithm

The salp swarm algorithm (SSA) is based on the swarm behavior of salps. This algorithmic technique often has a better performance than other swarm algorithms. SSA is a stochastic algorithm. At the start of the optimization process, the initial population is formed by creating a set of random solutions. These solutions improve over time in two stages— exploration and exploitation. In the exploration stage, the search space is explored. In exploitation, the neighborhood is exploited. By combining exploration with exploitation, the algorithm avoids getting trapped in local optima.

The position of the leader is updated in Equation 5-1.

$$X_j^1 = \begin{cases} F_j + c_1((ub_j - lb_j)c_2 + lb_j) & c_3 \geq 0 \\ F_j - c_1((ub_j - lb_j)c_2 + lb_j) & c_3 < 0 \end{cases}$$

Equation 5-1. *Position updating for salp swarms*

X_j^1 and F_j denote the positions of the leaders and the feeding sources in the jth dimension, respectively. The ub_j and lb_j indicate the jth dimension's upper (superior) and lower (inferior) bounds. c_2 and c_3 are two random floats from the closed interval [0, 1].

The coefficient, c_1, the most effective parameter in SSA, gradually decreases throughout iterations to balance exploration and exploitation, as defined in Equation 5-2.

$$c_1 = 2e^{-(4l\,L)(\text{pow})2}$$

Equation 5-2. *Coefficient c_1 calculation*

l and L represent the current iteration and the maximum number of iterations, respectively. Equation 5-3 updates the position of the followers.

$$X_j^i = \frac{X_j^i + X_j^{i-1}}{2}$$

Equation 5-3. *Position updating for followers*

Flowchart

Figure 5-1 is a flowchart of the salp swarm optimization algorithm. At a high level, this flowchart starts by initializing the parameters, such as the number of iterations and the population size. During each iteration, the positions of the leader and the followers are updated, and the fitness of each salp is calculated. After max iterations, the fittest solution is returned.

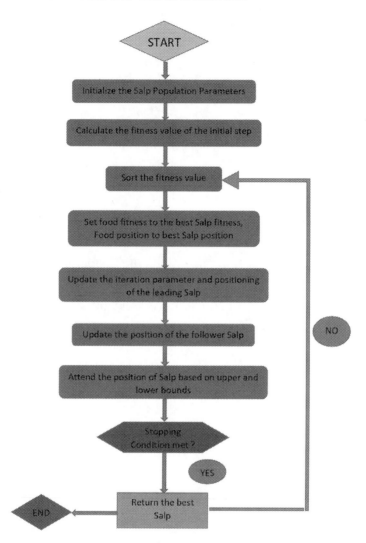

Figure 5-1. Flowchart for salp swarm optimization

Pseudocode

The following pseudocode describes the salp swarm optimization algorithm, as outlined in Figure 5-1.

```
Initialize the population of salps (i = 1, 2, .., n) considering
lower and upper bounds
    while (max iterations are not done)
    Calculate the fitness value of each salp
    Set F as the best salp
    Update the parameter c, using Eq (5.2)
        for salp
            f(i==1)
                Update the position of leader salp by Eq (5.1)
            else
                Update the position of follower salps by Eq (5.3)
            end
        end
    Update the position of salps considering lower and upper
    limits of variables end
return F
```

Prerequisites and Code

Make sure that Java 8 (JDK8 or higher) is installed on your computer. An IDE like Eclipse is recommended but not necessary because you can use the command-line interface to run the code without an IDE.

The code for the salp swarm optimizer algorithm contains the following classes.

- Point is the utility class with three members (see Listing 5-1).

  - A double array

- • An array of integers

- • An integer

- Rastrigin is the utility class for the optimization evaluation function (see Listing 5-2). The Rastrigin equation is shown in Equation 5-4.

- SalpSwarmOptimizer is the main optimizer class (see Listing 5-3). The objective function is the minimization of the benchmark function (Rastrigin in this case).

$$f(\mathbf{x}) = An + \sum_{i=1}^{n} \left[x_i^2 - A\cos(2\pi x_i) \right]$$

$$\text{where: } A = 10$$

Equation 5-4. *Rastrigin benchmark function*

Each listing contains detailed comments to more accurately describe specific sections of the code.

Listing 5-1. The Point Class

```
public class Point {
    public double p[];
    public int ip[];
    public int dim;

    public Point(double p[]) {
        this.dim = p.length;
        this.p = p.clone();
    }
```

```
public Point(int p[]) {
   this.dim = p.length;
   this.ip = p.clone();
}

public Point(int dim) {
   this.dim = dim;
   p = new double[dim];
}
/*
this method returns the square root of the sum of the
square of the members in the array of doubles
*/
public double norm(){
   double sum = 0;
   for (int i = 0; i < dim ; i ++) {
      sum += Math.pow(this.p[i], 2);
   }
   return Math.sqrt(sum);
}
/*
This method returns the square root of the distance between
2 points. Its calculated by taking sum of the square of the
distance between each element of the double array and then
doing a square root of it.
*/
public double dist(Point b){
   double sum = 0;
   for (int i = 0; i < dim ; i ++) {
      sum += Math.pow(this.p[i]-b.p[i], 2);
   }
```

```
    return Math.sqrt(sum);
}
/*
This method adds the two Points by taking sum of the
individual elements of the double array of each Point
*/

public static Point add(Point a, Point b) throws Exception {
    if (a.dim != b.dim){
        throw new IllegalArgumentException("Adding points
        from different dimensions");
    }
    int dim  = a.dim;
    double cp[] = new double[dim];
    for (int i = 0; i < dim; i++){
        cp[i] = a.p[i] + b.p[i];
    }
    return new Point(cp);
}
/*
This method adds the two Points by taking sum of the
individual elements of the double array of each Point and
then takes an average of each added elements and finally
returns a Point with the averages points in the new array
*/

public static Point mid(Point a, Point b) throws Exception{
    if (a.dim != b.dim){
        throw new IllegalArgumentException("Incompatible
        points");
    }
    int dim  = a.dim;
    double cor[] = new double[dim];
```

```
    for (int i = 0; i < dim; i++){
        cor[i] = (a.p[i] + b.p[i]) / 2.0;
    }
    return new Point (cor);
}
/*
This method multiplies each element of the array of double
with the constant a. a is the coefficient we use in the
optimization algorithm.
*/
public Point mull(double a) {
    double p[] = new double[this.dim];
    Point m = new Point(p);
    for (int i = 0; i < this.dim; i++){
        m.p[i] = this.p[i]*a;
    }
    return m;
}
/*
This method returns a string representation of the double
array
*/

@Override
public String toString() {
    if (p != null) {
        String s = "[";
        for (int i = 0; i < this.dim; i++){
            s += (float)p[i];
            if (i == this.dim - 1) {
                s += "]";
```

```
        } else {
            s += ",";
        }
    }
    return s;
} else {
    String s = "[";
    for (int i = 0; i < this.dim; i++){
        s += (int)ip[i];
        if (i == this.dim - 1) {
            s += "]";
        } else {
            s += ",";
        }
    }
    return s;
    }
  }
}
```

Listing 5-2. The Rastrigin Class

```
/*
This class is used as the benchmark function and will be
used throughout all algorithms.
*/

public class Rastrigin {

    private double A;
    private double n;
```

```java
public Rastrigin(double A, double n) {
    this.A = A;
    this.n = n;
}

/*
This method is the main method for the Rastrigin benchmark
function. It takes as input a Point object (explained
above) and performs the calculations for the benchmark.
*/

public double f(Point x) {
    double sum = 0;
    //o = numpy.sum(x ** 2 - 10 * numpy.cos
    (2 * math.pi * x)) + 10 * dim
    for (int i = 0; i < x.dim; i++) {

        sum += Math.pow(x.p[i], 2) - A*Math.cos
        (2*Math.PI*x.p[i]);

    }
    return A*n + sum;
}

}
```

Listing 5-3. The SalpSwarmOptimizer Class

```java
/*
This class is the main optimizer class . Our objective function
is the minimization of the benchmark function (Rastrigin in
this case)
*/
```

```java
import java.lang.Math;
import java.util.*;
public class SalpSwarmOptimizer
{
// declare variables for population size, number of iterations,
    dimensions and bounds.

int popSize;
int iterations;

int dimensions;
//declaration of bounds
double ub=5.12,lb=-5.12;
//array for holding the fitness values
double fitness[];
double[] bestSolution;

double minValueOfSolution;
double[][] positions;

public SalpSwarmOptimizer(int iterations,int popSize, int
dimensions)
{
    this.iterations=iterations;
    this.popSize=popSize;
    this.dimensions=dimensions;
    positions=new double[popSize][dimensions];
    fitness=new double[popSize];
    //initialize solutions

    for(int i=0;i<popSize;i++)
    {
    for (int j=0;j<dimensions;j++)
    {

        double rnd=Math.random();
```

```java
        positions[i][j]=rnd*(ub-lb)+lb;
    }
    }

    for(int i=0;i<popSize;i++)
    {
        fitness[i]=fitnessCalculator(positions[i]);

    }
    int bestIndex= indexOfSmallest(fitness);

    bestSolution=positions[bestIndex];

    minValueOfSolution=fitness[bestIndex];

}
//rastrigin function used
private  double fitnessCalculator(double[] candidate)
{

    Point p= new Point(candidate);
    Rastrigin rast=new Rastrigin(10,dimensions);
    return rast.f(p);

}
/*
Helper method which finds the index of the smallest member in
an array of doubles
*/

private static int indexOfSmallest(double[] array){

    // add this
    if (array.length == 0)
        return -1;
```

```
    int index = 0;
    double min = array[index];

    for (int i = 1; i < array.length; i++){
        if (array[i] <= min){
        min = array[i];
        index = i;
        }
    }
    return index;
}
/*
Helper method to do a matrix transpose
*/

private double[][] transpose(double[][] original ,int rows, int
columns)
{

    double[][] transpose=new double[rows][columns];
    for(int i=0;i<rows;i++){
for(int j=0;j<columns;j++){

transpose[i][j]=original[j][i];
}
}
return transpose;
}
/*
Helper method to return rows for a specific column of the matrix
*/
```

```
private double[] getRows(double[][] arr,int colIndex)
{
    double[] result=new double[arr.length]; //size is number
                                             of rows

    for(int i=0;i<arr.length;i++)
    {
        for (int col = 0; col < arr[i].length; col++) {

        if(col==colIndex)
        {

        result[i]=arr[i][col];
        }

        }
    }
    return result;
}
/*
Helper method which adds element of two dimensional each array
and returns a two dimensional array
*/

private  double[][] addElementwise(double[] a, double[]
b,double[][] positions,int dim, int pop) throws
ArithmeticException {
        if (a.length != b.length) {
            throw new ArithmeticException();
        } else {
            for (int i = 0; i < a.length; i++) {
                positions[dim][pop] = ((a[i] + b[i])/2);
            }
```

```java
        return positions;
    }

  }

/*
Method for running the iterations and optimizer code
*/

private void optimize()
{
    //main loop

    for(int i=0;i<iterations;i++){

        double c1 = 2 * Math.exp(-(Math.pow(4 * i /
        iterations,2)));
        //loop over individual moth
        for(int j=0;j<popSize;j++)
        {
            // perform a matrix transform
            positions =transpose(positions,dimensions,
            popSize);

            if (j < popSize/2)
            {
              for (int k=0;k<dimensions;k++)
                {
                double c2 = Math.random();
                double c3 = Math.random();
        // update the position at kth row and jth column based
           on value of c1 and c2
```

```
    if (c3 < 0.5)
    {
        positions[k][j] = bestSolution[k] +
        c1 * ((ub - lb) * c2 + lb);

        }
    else
        {
        positions[k][j] = bestSolution[k] -
        c1 * ((ub - lb) * c2 + lb);

        }
    }
}

else if ((j >= popSize / 2) && (j < popSize + 1)){
    double[] point1= getRows(positions,j-1);

  double[] point2 = getRows(positions,j);

    for (int k=0;k<dimensions;k++)
    {
    positions=addElementwise(point1,point2,
    positions,k,j);

    }

}
// transpose the matrix back for next iteration
positions = transpose(positions,popSize,dimensions);

}

for(int j=0;j<popSize;j++)
{
    positions[j]=simpleBounds(positions[j],lb,ub);
```

```
        // calculate fitness of each salp swarm
      double fNew = fitnessCalculator(positions[j]);

        // Update the current best solution
      if (fNew < minValueOfSolution)
        {
          bestSolution =positions[j].clone();
          minValueOfSolution = fNew;

        }

      }
      System.out.println("minimum value at iterartion
      "+i+"="+minValueOfSolution);
    }

}
/*
Method for bounding the value between lower and upper bounds
*/
private double[] simpleBounds(double[] val, double lower,
double upper){
    double[] result = new double[val.length];
    for (int i = 0; i < val.length; i++) {

        if (val[i] < lower){
            result[i] = lower;

        }
        else if (val[i] > upper){
            result[i] = upper;
```

```java
        }
        else
        {
            result[i]=val[i];

        }

    }

        return result;
}
/*
Main method to pass inputs and launch the algorithm
*/

public static void main(String[] args)
{
//takes input as number of iterations, population size and
dimensions

int iter=Integer.parseInt(args[0]);
int pop=Integer.parseInt(args[1]);
int dim=Integer.parseInt(args[2]);
SalpSwarmOptimizer swarm =new SalpSwarmOptimizer(iter,pop,dim);
swarm.optimize();
}

}
```

Executing the Code

Let's compile the source code and execute it. The following are the commands for compiling the Java files.

```
javac Point.java
javac Rastrigin.java
javac SalpSwarmOptimizer.java

//running the example with 50 iterations and population size of
10 and 30 dimensions
java SalpSwarmOptimizer 50 10 30
```

Output

After executing the code, you see the following results.

```
minimum value at iterartion 0=244.86356621486414
minimum value at iterartion 1=124.07861122372111
minimum value at iterartion 2=45.215002332220735
minimum value at iterartion 3=45.215002332220735
minimum value at iterartion 4=10.8885992360552
minimum value at iterartion 5=10.8885992360552
minimum value at iterartion 6=10.8885992360552
minimum value at iterartion 7=10.8885992360552
minimum value at iterartion 8=10.8885992360552
minimum value at iterartion 9=10.8885992360552
minimum value at iterartion 10=10.8885992360552
minimum value at iterartion 11=10.8885992360552
minimum value at iterartion 12=10.8885992360552
minimum value at iterartion 13=10.8885992360552
minimum value at iterartion 14=10.8885992360552
minimum value at iterartion 15=10.8885992360552
```

```
minimum value at iterartion 16=10.8885992360552
minimum value at iterartion 17=10.8885992360552
minimum value at iterartion 18=10.8885992360552
minimum value at iterartion 19=10.8885992360552
minimum value at iterartion 20=10.8885992360552
minimum value at iterartion 21=0.29297658145605965
minimum value at iterartion 22=0.29297658145605965
minimum value at iterartion 23=0.29297658145605965
minimum value at iterartion 24=0.29297658145605965
minimum value at iterartion 25=0.29297658145605965
minimum value at iterartion 26=0.29297658145605965
minimum value at iterartion 27=0.29297658145605965
minimum value at iterartion 28=0.29297658145605965
minimum value at iterartion 29=0.29297658145605965
minimum value at iterartion 30=0.29297658145605965
minimum value at iterartion 31=0.29297658145605965
minimum value at iterartion 32=0.29297658145605965
minimum value at iterartion 33=0.29297658145605965
minimum value at iterartion 34=0.29297658145605965
minimum value at iterartion 35=0.29297658145605965
minimum value at iterartion 36=0.29297658145605965
minimum value at iterartion 37=0.29297658145605965
minimum value at iterartion 38=0.28874178108526394
minimum value at iterartion 39=0.28857296330363624
minimum value at iterartion 40=0.2515754513162278
minimum value at iterartion 41=0.2433592726172833
minimum value at iterartion 42=0.1984760429712651
minimum value at iterartion 43=0.18909883434662333
minimum value at iterartion 44=0.17737272169620155
minimum value at iterartion 45=0.1590004357810244
```

```
minimum value at iterartion 46=0.14865231084121433
minimum value at iterartion 47=0.14865231084121433
minimum value at iterartion 48=0.14865231084121433
minimum value at iterartion 49=0.12695612866474448
```

Summary

This chapter introduced optimization problem solutions specific to salp swarms and their foraging behavior. It covered the basic flow of the optimization problem and solution, the flowchart, pseudocode, and code written in Java. The Rastrigin benchmark function was used as the objective function in the algorithms.

Index

A, B

Bats optimization
  BatOptimizer class, 62, 68–70,
    72, 73, 75
  code execution, 77, 78
  dimensions, 58
  echolocation, 57, 58
  flowchart, 59, 60
  Point class, 62–64, 66
  position/velocity, 59
  pseudocode, 61
  Rastrigin class, 62, 66, 67
Benchmark functions, 10, 93, 108
Birds
  cognitive component, 83
  flocking, 81, 82
  rules, 82
  social component, 83
Black-box optimization techniques,
    see Metaheuristic
    techniques
Brood parasitism, 101, 102
Bubble-net attacking
    method, 16
Bubble-net feeding
    method, 14

C, D

Cuckoo search optimization (CSO)
  assumptions, 104
  behaviors
    brood parasitism, 101, 102
    Lévy flight, 102, 103
  code execution, 124
  CuckooSearch class,
    115, 117–123
  CuckooSearchDataHolder
    class, 108, 114
  flowchart, 105, 106
  Lévy function, 105
  output, 124, 125
  Point class, 108–112
  population of solutions, 104
  pseudocode, 107
  Rastrigin class, 108, 113
  step size, 105

E

Emergence, 5–7
Emergent behaviors, 6, 7
Exact optimization methods, 3
Exploration *vs.* Exploitation, 8

© Shashank Jain 2022
S. Jain, *Nature-Inspired Optimization Algorithms with Java*,
https://doi.org/10.1007/978-1-4842-7401-9

Printed in the United States
by Baker & Taylor Publisher Services